THE 2 MEAL DAY

Burn fat and boost energy through intermittent fasting

MAX LOWERY

Photography by Kate Whitaker and Michelle Beatty

KYLE BOOKS

To my dad, Philip, for sparking my interest in food and my mother, Romaine, for pushing me to pursue my passion.

Published in 2018 by Kyle Books
www.kylebooks.com

Distributed by National Book Network
4501 Forbes Blvd, Suite 200,
Lanham, MD 20706
Phone: (800) 462-6420
Fax: (800) 338-4550
customercare@nbnbooks.com

First published in Great Britain in 2017
by Kyle Books
an imprint of Kyle Cathie Limited

10 9 8 7 6 5 4 3 2 1
ISBN 978-1-909487-81-9
Library of Congress Control Number: 2017950937

Editor: Vicky Orchard
Editorial Adaptation: Christy Lusiak
Design: Tania Gomes
Photography: Kate Whitaker and Michelle Beatty
Food styling: Annie Rigg
Props styling: Jo Harris
Production: Lisa Pinnell
Color reproduction by ALTA London
Printed and bound in China by 1010 International Printing Ltd.

Thank Yous

I would like to thank my parents for the opportunities they gave me. My girlfriend Lylah, for her support and understanding. Zac, for his help and ideas. My sprint coach, Peter Griffiths, for teaching me so much. And Alistair for making things happen!

Thanks to Kate Whitaker, Annie Rigg, and Jo Harris for the delicious food photos, Michelle Beatty for the brilliant exercise photos, and Tania Gomes for her book design. I would also like thank Dr. Adam Collins for his hugely helpful feedback and comments on the text.

Disclaimer

CONTENTS

Introduction   4

Why two meals are better

than three   8

Recipes   20

Higher carb   36

Lower carb   72

Healthier snacks   132

Healthier desserts   150

Exercise   168

Index   190

THE **2** MEAL DAY

I started intermittent fasting (IF) completely unintentionally while traveling through South America. I was trying to live as cheaply as possible, so I only ate one massive meal a day at the same time as training hard and going on 6 to 8-hour hikes up mountains at least once a week. When I got home I weighed myself: 175 pounds; 6 percent body fat; 160 pounds muscle mass. I'd lost an incredible 15 pounds, yet I was more muscular than I had ever been. I then returned to my normal routine, however, eating three big (low-carb) meals a day, which meant I quickly put the weight back on. I have never had any problems building or maintaining muscle, but I just wasn't as lean as I was when I was away.

Without realizing it, in South America I had been following a type of IF. Intermittent fasting just means breaking up your day or week into eating and non-eating periods. By eating one meal a day I was fasting for up to 20 hours. After further research I decided to experiment with a daily fast, which I called the 2-Meal Day (2MD). I skipped breakfast and ate just lunch and dinner, so that I was fasting for 16-18 hours every day. I found the 2MD the simplest, most effective way to lose weight and reap the many benefits of fasting—no calorie counting, obsessing over when to eat, or feelings of deprivation: the two meals I did eat were big and very satisfying.

Initially, I thought that this way of eating would be a struggle. I was someone who always "needed" to eat breakfast and used to think my whole world would collapse if I didn't have my eggs in the morning. However, it was surprisingly easy and within a few days I really got into the swing of it.

Almost effortlessly and very quickly I became leaner and visibly lost body fat without losing any muscle mass. To my surprise I was actually less hungry than before. I stopped constantly thinking about my next meal or worrying if I wasn't going to have time to have breakfast or lunch. An added bonus was that as well as time, I was saving money as I was no longer buying a substandard, unsatisfying breakfast grabbed from whichever sandwich shop was nearest.

The most useful benefit I discovered (aside from fat loss) was the stabilization of my energy levels. Digestion actually takes up a lot of energy, and by fasting and freeing that up, you can get a real "buzz." Before the 2MD I would start "crashing" between breakfast and lunch (even with a low-carb diet). Now my energy levels are constant all day, even without any caffeine.

As a personal trainer I regularly have back-to-back clients from 7am to 4pm. My fellow trainers think I am crazy

NO CALORIE COUNTING, OBSESSING OVER WHEN TO EAT, OR FEELINGS OF DEPRIVATION

when they find out I don't have breakfast before work, but with the 2MD I don't once think about food or feel tired during the sessions.

My clients who have tried the 2MD using my online plans have had great results, not only with weight loss, but also giving them back control over their own bodies. They no longer feel hungry all the time or spend time constantly thinking about their next meal.

This way of eating restores the body to its natural state—burning stored body fat for energy. We are naturally fat burners, but because fat is essential for our survival, our body will choose to burn the sugars from food if we are constantly eating. This is a reminder of how our bodies haven't really changed since we were hunter-gatherers. On the rare occasion there would be a surplus of food, our bodies would cling on to our fat reserves in preparation for harsher times. Only when there was a lack of food would we start burning that stored energy. Now there is a constant supply of food, but our bodies haven't adjusted to this new environment, and we still cling on to our fat reserves in preparation for the next difficult period.

Following the 2-Meal Day effectively tricks your body into thinking there isn't any food available, so you start burning stored body fat for energy. That's not all though, hormones are then released to make you better at catching your next meal, your energy levels and mental alertness increase, coordination and body movements improve, and you stop feeling hungry.

After four years following the 2MD I am stronger, leaner, faster, healthier, richer, and more efficient than I've ever been. The 2MD is not just a diet, it's a lifestyle that has become a crucial part of my health and fitness journey.

I truly believe that intermittent fasting is the missing link in our overall health and well-being, and the 2MD is the simplest, most effective method to reap the rewards. It's my goal to share my method with as many people as possible!

CHAPTER 1

WHY TWO MEALS ARE BETTER THAN THREE

After four years of experimenting with different methods of intermittent fasting, I have come up with the simplest, most effective way to burn fat, boost energy, and banish hunger: no calorie counting, obsessing over eating windows, or feelings of deprivation—just two meals a day. You will eat two meals and one optional healthy snack in between those meals every day.

WHAT IS INTERMITTENT FASTING?

Intermittent fasting (or more accurately intermittent energy restriction) is a general term for various eating patterns that involve fasting for short periods of time. Unlike a typical weight-loss diet that restricts how much or what you eat, intermittent fasting within a 24-hour period, like the 2MD, is all about integrating periods of fasting into your day to reap the many proven benefits, including burning stored body fat for energy, feeling less hungry, and improving overall health. This is slightly different to alternate day fasting, or variants such as the 5:2 diet, where fasting is restricted to specific days rather than incorporated into every day.

THE HISTORY OF EATING

The Western world has only been eating three meals a day—breakfast (early morning), lunch (early afternoon), and dinner (evening)—for 400 years or so. This may seem like a long time but homo sapiens (us) have been around for 200,000 years. Only in the last 10,000 years have we been cultivating the land for agricultural purposes (before that we were hunter-gatherers and had to go out and catch our food on a daily basis), and only since the Industrial Revolution in the eighteenth century has there been a more or less consistent surplus of food.

So, for most of our history eating three meals a day was neither necessary nor possible and early humans and certain indigenous people like the Native Americans ate when they were hungry, rather than being slaves to the clock or blood-sugar fluctuations. Eating three meals a day is not based on our biological needs but started due to cultural reasons.

According to food historian Caroline Yeldham, the Romans believed it was healthier to eat only one meal a day. They were very aware of the process of digestion and recognized the benefits of giving the digestive system a break. Equally, in the fifteenth and sixteenth centuries during the European colonization of the Americas, Native American communities consumed food in small portions throughout the day and sometimes fasted by choice for days at a time to cleanse and heal their bodies for rituals. European settlers took their lack of defined eating times as evidence that they were uncivilized and made them change their eating patterns to three square meals a day.

In medieval Europe, breakfast was a luxury reserved for the rich. Most people couldn't afford to indulge in the practice and skipped it since it wasn't necessary. Historians tend to agree that breakfast became a part of daily routine once workers moved to cities and became employees who worked set schedules. In Europe, this began in the 1600s and became the norm during the Industrial Revolution.

Only relatively recently has there been emphasis on breakfast as the most important meal of the day. At the turn of the twentieth century the first mass-produced, processed-food product

> FOR MOST OF OUR HISTORY EATING THREE MEALS A DAY WAS NEITHER NECESSARY NOR POSSIBLE

was created—breakfast cereal. In 1895 John Harvey Kellogg launched the Cornflakes brand, which captured a national market thanks to an extensive advertising campaign. He succeeded in transforming agricultural surplus—leftover degraded grains—into a profitable product.

Cereal was the first heavily marketed food product. In 1944 a campaign was launched by Grape Nuts manufacturer, General Foods, to sell more cereal. During the campaign, which marketers named "Eat a Good Breakfast—Do a Better Job," grocery stores handed out pamphlets that promoted the importance of breakfast while radio advertisements announced that: "Nutrition experts say breakfast is the most important meal of the day." In fact, the little nutritional value the grains used in cereals may once have had was destroyed during processing, so manufacturers began to fortify their products by spraying them with artificial nutrients.

But the cereal marketing strategies were so successful that almost everyone I speak to on the subject repeats the same two myths, namely that breakfast is the most important meal of the day and/or skipping breakfast slows down your metabolism, even though there is virtually no scientific evidence to back up these claims.

Professor James Betts, who specializes in nutrition and metabolism at the University of Bath (UK), carried out a meta-analysis, combining data from multiple studies on the effect of eating breakfast on weight loss. His conclusion: "The problem is that these benefits of eating breakfast, although logical sounding, are largely assumptions based on observational studies and have never actually been tested." Observational studies are not carried out in controlled environments and don't take into consideration any other factors, such as activity levels or whether people smoke. "I was amazed when I started looking for evidence—I thought there would be a lot," he said.

So, there is little direct evidence to support eating breakfast as an important start to the day. This doesn't mean that you shouldn't eat it if you want to, but it does mean that you shouldn't feel that you have to eat breakfast or that skipping it will have a negative impact on your health.

Since the invention of breakfast cereal the processed-food industry has exploded. Companies are constantly trying to sell us their "food-like" products, such as cereal bars and snacks that are nutritionally sparse and highly

profitable. Snacking culture has become the norm and now any time of day is a time to eat. We "graze" all day, typically eating over a long period of 12 hours or more, becoming totally out of touch with our natural body clocks. This is having a negative effect on our waistlines, energy levels, and overall health and well-being.

Fasting is not a new idea—almost every ancient civilization and religion knew that it was a powerful tool for cleansing and healing the body—but due to our modern snacking culture and the marketing campaigns of massive food corporations (in 2013 the food and beverage industry in the US alone spent $1.36 billion on advertising) we have completely lost sight of the fact that fasting was used for healing throughout ancient history. Hippocrates, referred to as the father of modern medicine, endorsed the practice of fasting, as did Ancient Greek thinkers such as Plato and his student Aristotle. Hippocrates famously wrote: "Our food should be our medicine. Our medicine should be our food. But to eat when you are sick is to feed your sickness." He recognized that food could be the source of some of our illnesses and that fasting could have a positive effect on our health and well-being. So far from being some kind of radical new approach, the 2MD is more of a return to a natural way of eating.

BREAKFAST OR DINNER?

When following the 2-Meal Day you need to choose between eating breakfast and lunch or lunch and dinner. Your first step is to decide

which meal you are going to skip. Although it may seem minor, this choice has a big impact on your ability to stick to the plan. Both options mean you are fasting for between 16 and 18 hours, but depending on your schedule and personal preference you may find that one is preferable and easier to implement than the other. If you are someone who finds it difficult to eat later in the evening, then it might be best to skip dinner and eat breakfast and lunch. Once you have picked which two meals you are eating, try to stick with your decision and be consistent.

Eating lunch and dinner and skipping breakfast is most effective for me. It's also much simpler to implement socially because you are more likely to eat lunch and dinner with friends and family. It also means you have extra time in the morning to get a little more sleep or do the stretching/mobility sequence on page 173. After eating the parasympathetic nervous system is stimulated. Parasympathetic neurones drive activities that occur when the body is at rest. Sometimes called the "rest-and-digest" system, it increases energy consumption for digestive activity. This can be the cause of the sluggish, lethargic feeling you can sometimes experience after eating, particularly if you've eaten a rich meal, high in protein, fiber, and complex carbohydrate. Surely it makes more sense to save this feeling for later in the day, once all your daily tasks have been completed?

THE BENEFITS OF FASTING

Fasting, as we have seen, is not a new idea, having been practiced by virtually every ancient culture and religion to cleanse and heal the body for rituals. But what are the benefits?

Weight loss

About 4 to 5 hours after we finish eating, our insulin levels (the hormone response for lowering blood sugar) have fallen and the newly delivered carbohydrate is dealt with, which coincides with a series of hormonal changes as we enter a fasted state. The body will then make the transition towards burning fat for energy. We need a certain amount of body fat to survive, but if we are constantly fed and absorbing the energy from our food then our bodies will only burn glucose/glycogen (stored carbohydrate) for energy and never really rely heavily on fat for fuel. If we don't use up our constant supply and stores of carbohydrate through exercise and activity then our bodies never get better at burning fat for energy.

We need to give our bodies the chance to use fat as it is designed to be used, as a back-up fuel, by not constantly supplying them with food. Getting the body to burn fat rather glucose for energy is key to most of the health benefits of fasting and why it can be so effective as a weight-loss tool. Fasting has also been shown to help significantly decrease visceral fat—the dangerous fat stored around the belly and internal organs—which is a risk factor for Type 2 diabetes, heart disease, breast cancer, colorectal cancer, and Alzheimer's.

Stable energy levels

Fat can be used as a significant fuel source for everyday activities. However, you have to create the right conditions to burn fat for energy. If you are constantly eating, your body will prefer to use fuel from the carbohydrates you consume rather than turning to fat for energy. High GI food and drinks (those high in free sugars) may give you a short, sharp spike in energy, but you will quickly crash again. If you constantly reach for external substances to give you energy, your body will just use this fuel you supply.

Digestion actually takes up a lot of energy (hence that lethargic feeling after eating a meal), so during your fasting hours you are freeing up that energy to power the brain

INTERMITTENT
FASTING HAS BEEN
USED TO CLEANSE
AND HEAL THE BODY
FOR THOUSANDS
OF YEARS

and muscles. Additionally, a hormone called norepinephrine is released, which has been shown to have a positive effect on mental alertness, so much so that some people report feeling a buzz from fasting.

Reduced hunger

People are often surprised that reduced hunger is a benefit of fasting. After the initial transitional period when your body gets used to a new way of eating, you find yourself thinking about food less. Fasting normalizes your hunger hormones (ghrelin) and improves your sensitivity to leptin (an appetite suppressant hormone) allowing you to feel real hunger which occurs every 16 to 24 hours. This is one of the most empowering benefits. You become self-sufficient, no longer counting down the minutes until you can next eat; you are in tune with your

body. When the body is temporarily freed from digestion for 16 to 18 hours, it's also able to focus its regenerative abilities.

Improved insulin sensitivity

If your diet regularly raises your blood sugar, then your body constantly has to secrete insulin to bring those sugar levels back down. Your body reacts to insulin in a similar way it would to a drug—you don't need much to feel its effects at first, but after a while you start to need more and more to have the same effect as your body becomes less responsive to it. This is known as "insulin resistance," and is a contributing factor to Type 2 diabetes and a whole host of other conditions, such as obesity, cardiovascular disease and stroke, high blood pressure, kidney disease, and Alzheimer's.

Currently, about 6 percent of the UK population have Type 2 diabetes, rising to 10 percent in the US, but it has been estimated that by 2050 the figure could be as high as 20 percent. If you constantly eat all day, your body has to keep releasing insulin to control the blood-sugar fluctuations. Fasting gets your body to become more insulin sensitive by decreasing these blood-sugar fluctuations.

Reduced risk of cancer, Alzheimer's, and heart disease

In 2016 the Nobel Prize in Physiology went to Yoshinori Ohsumi for discovering the working mechanisms for a process called autophagy, which means "self-eating" in Greek. That may sound terrible, but actually it is a highly beneficial process. It is essentially your body's recycling system. Your cells create membranes that probe for scraps of dead, diseased, or worn-out cells. They cannibalize them and use the resulting molecules for energy or to make new cell parts. This process can slow cancerous growths and stop metabolic dysfunction like obesity and diabetes, which are both contributors to heart disease. Fasting and exercise are the most effective methods at inducing autophagy since it only occurs in the fasted state (see fasted exercise, pages 17–18).

Slowing of the aging process

Scientists have known since the 1930s that if they want to increase the lifespan of test rats, they put them on an intermittent fasting schedule like the alternate-day fasting method, whereby they eat normally one day and then fast the next. Test rats that ate exactly the same amount of food as other rats but were fed intermittently have been shown to outlive rats that ate normally. Although this is far from being proven in humans, intermittent fasting has become very popular among the anti-aging movement. Given the known benefits for metabolism and all sorts of health markers, it makes sense that intermittent fasting could help you live a longer and healthier life.

Improved immune system

Fasting not only protects against damage to the immune system, but also induces its regeneration, shifting stem cells from a dormant state to one of self-renewal (see left).

FASTED EXERCISE

You may think you need food to fuel your workouts, but you are wrong. For years the advice has been to load up on carbohydrates before exercise and keep topping off during exercise, but more recently this has been questioned (particularly if you're not exercising at a competitive level). Consuming carbs before (and during) exercise can increase performance in certain fields, such as sprinting and sports that use power movements, but "fueling up" will limit the depletion of fuel (carbs) stored in the muscles for energy, so you are less likely to burn fat over time and therefore less likely to reap the weight-loss benefits of exercise.

During the day you go in and out of fed and fasted states. The fed state lasts about 4 to 6 hours after your last meal. Insulin is released to take up glucose from the blood, proteins and fats are absorbed by the digestive system, and in the muscle glucose is burnt as fuel and/or stored as energy (glycogen).

Six hours after eating you enter the fasted state. Glucagon is released to keep your blood sugar at normal levels. Your body starts to break down adipose (fat) tissue into free fatty acids, which are used for energy in the muscles and other peripheral tissues. Being in the fasted state for several hours eventually leads to reliance on a process called ketosis where the fatty acids are converted into ketones by the liver to substitute for glucose when the carbohydrate stores run out. When you start eating again, insulin inhibits the breakdown of fatty acids into usable energy, as your body shifts to utilizing carbs once again, essentially decreasing this fat-burning mechanism.

This makes perfect evolutionary sense; body fat is part of our metabolic coping with "feast and famine," particularly the latter when food wasn't as readily available as it is today. Now food is in almost constant supply but our bodies are still physiologically the same as they were tens of thousands of years ago. If we eat all day, we never tap into our bodies' natural ability to burn stored body fat for energy. Fasted exercise can maximize this potential even further.

I have trained fasted for four years now, and for three of those I was a competitive sprinter, competing nationally in the 100m, 200m, and 400m. I hate the feeling of training with food in my stomach; I feel heavy, bloated, and lethargic. When competing I followed the "train low, compete high" principle. I trained fasted, allowing my body to become as efficient as possible at maximizing energy reserves and then at competitions I raced with high carbohydrate stores to maximize performance.

Initially, your workouts will feel a lot harder than usual when you train in a fasted state, but after two weeks or so your body will become more efficient as your muscles learn to use less glycogen, which means you will use fatty acids for fuel instead. Push through the initial transition period and you will soon reap the weight-loss benefits of fasted training.

BUSTING FASTING MYTHS

People sometimes have reservations about intermittent fasting, largely due to a lot of misinformation about its effects. Here are the three most common misconceptions:

Myth #1: fasting slows down your metabolism

In fact, the opposite is true. Lower insulin levels, higher growth-hormone levels, and increased amounts of norepinephrine all increase the breakdown of body fat and facilitate its use for energy. So, short-term fasting actually increases your metabolic rate by 3.6 to 14 percent, helping you burn slightly more calories. More importantly, it also increases the amount of fat that is burnt for energy, contributing to loss of body fat and overall weight loss. Studies suggest that only after 72 hours of fasting does your metabolism start to slow down.

Myth #2: fasting = starvation

There is a vast difference between fasting and starving. Starvation is total abstention from food for several days and is when the body is forced to use vital tissue to survive.

The goal of fasting is not to calorie restrict, but to restrict meal frequency by extending the time between the last meal one day and the first meal the next. On the 2MD you are just eating your first meal a few hours later if you are a breakfast skipper or having your last meal of the day earlier if you cut out dinner. When you eat, you eat until you are full, enjoying every bite!

Myth #3: your muscles will waste away

One of the main benefits of fasting is the effect on growth hormone (GH) in the blood, which can increase by up to five times. Higher levels of GH facilitate fat-burning, muscle building, and prevent muscle wastage when supported by the nutrients provided by your two meals.

CHAPTER 2

RECIPES

In this chapter I will explain my food philosophy, the role of macronutrients, and my thoughts on supplements. Then we'll look at some of the more practical aspects of the 2-Meal Day, plus how to overcome some of the obstacles you may encounter. Lastly, it is important to think about how alcohol fits in with the 2MD.

MY PHILOSOPHY

My food philosophy is simple: eat locally sourced, seasonal foods full of nutrients. In other words, eat real food. The body is not designed to constantly digest and metabolize food, particularly during inactive periods, and once you start eating foods that nourish your body you quickly realize that you don't need to eat every 3 to 4 hours. You begin to recognize what real hunger feels like, empowering yourself with the ability to become self-sufficient. You will never be a slave to mealtimes again!

Our bodies are naturally fat-burning machines, but because of clever marketing and an abundance of food-like products, we have become dependent on sugar to supply us with energy. These food-like products are designed to have the perfect combination of sugar, salt, and/or fat so that they are highly desirable, leading to overconsumption and causing us to become fat and sick. Eating "little and often" or "grazing" has become the social norm, feeding the myth that it keeps the metabolism firing. We are encouraged to snack in between meals by companies creating products that are cheap, nutrient sparse, and highly processed.

It takes time for the body to adjust to a new way of eating, and it may be difficult for some people. It varies from person to person, but from my experience with clients it takes 1 to 2 weeks. If you find the first couple of weeks difficult, I can assure you it is worth persevering. Once your body starts using stored body fat for energy you will quickly burn fat, boost energy, and banish hunger.

Eat real food

Real food is a simple concept; it's what nature has given us: plants, fruits, roots, nuts, seeds, meat, fish, eggs, milk, and its by-products, such as cheese and yogurt. Real food is kept as close to its natural state as possible. It comes from animals that have led healthy, happy lives and that haven't been pumped full of hormones, steroids, and antibiotics, which are all transferred into the food chain. It should be minimally processed, not human-made, and it certainly shouldn't have a list of ingredients that you can't pronounce. If we weren't eating it 200 years ago, it probably doesn't qualify as real food.

A big factor in the current obesity, diabetes, and heart disease epidemic is that many of us are not eating real food any more. Instead, we are eating food-like products that may have started out as real food, but for the purposes of shelf life and/or profit have gone through processes that destroy the nutritional value they may once have had. These include things like cereal, cereal bars, chips, cookies, fizzy drinks, and chocolate bars, to name a few. We haven't evolved to digest these food-like products, and they are causing us to become fat, sick, and addicted to sugar. Next time you go shopping, notice how many food-like products there are—they take up most of the aisles!

Eating real food is fundamental to the 2-Meal Day. Start looking at food in terms of its nutritional content rather than calorific value (often the healthiest real foods contain the most calories). Since you will be eating two meals rather than three, it is crucial that the foods you eat are packed full of nutrients. My recipes are designed to be as nutritious as possible and to provide you with the macronutrients you need to achieve your goals.

MACRONUTRIENTS

Nutrients are substances used for energy, growth, and bodily functions. Macronutrients are those needed in larger amounts, and there are three types: fat, protein, and carbohydrates. Understanding the role that each plays in our bodily functions is fundamental to us making good food choices in our day-to-day lives.

Fat

A landmark study almost 50 years ago by scientist Ancel Keyes sent governments, the food industry, and the media down the wrong path, demonizing saturated fat and prompting the creation of a whole industry of low-fat products marketed as a healthier way to eat. Thirty years of increasing obesity, diabetes, and other metabolic diseases suggest that the answer is not that simple. Fortunately, there are hundreds of reputable studies and countless doctors and researchers recognizing that eating fat, particularly monounsaturated fat from plants sources such avocados and olive oil and polyunsaturated fat and omega-3 fatty acids from oily fish like salmon and mackerel are crucial to support optimum function for all the systems in the body.

Fat is a supplementary fuel source for all our vital organs (other than the brain), and is used during long-duration, low/medium intensity activities, such as walking, working, sleeping, and general everyday chores. Not only does excess carbohydrate intake stop you from using fat for these activities (which will cause fluctuations in energy levels) but the unused carbs can then be stored as fat. Eating a diet high in fat, with moderate protein consumption and eliminating "bad" carbohydrates, such as cakes, cookies, sweets, and fizzy drinks, means you generally reduce your overall calorie intake and are less likely to passively overconsume food overall.

> THE 2-MEAL DAY IS NOT A HIGH-PROTEIN DIET LIKE THE ATKINS OR DUKAN DIETS

Not all fats are equal, however. Hydrogenated fats (trans fats) are the unnatural highly processed fats found in cakes, cookies, pastries, low-fat products, and margarine. These should be avoided at all costs. They are entirely human-made, created in an industrial process that adds hydrogen to liquid vegetable oils to make them more solid. They have been shown to increase your LDL (bad cholesterol) and decrease your HDL (good cholesterol), which can massively increase the risk of developing heart disease and Alzheimer's.

Protein

Your body needs protein for growth and maintenance. It is one of the main building blocks in every cell, especially in your muscles, and, after water, it is the most abundant substance in your body. Additionally, protein contributes to the production of hormones and the regulation of metabolism. Eating protein will also keep you fuller for longer by stimulating the release of satiety hormones from the gut and because it takes longer to transit through the gut, get digested, and be absorbed by the body, protein doesn't create the spikes in blood-sugar levels that carbohydrates do.

It's important to point out that the 2-Meal Day is not a high-protein diet like the Atkins or Dukan diets. Very high-protein diets can put a strain on your kidneys, and are completely unnecessary for anyone other than professional athletes. Plus, protein can also be used by your body as a form of energy, so if you are eating too much it will stop you from being able to burn stored body fat. The aim here is to keep your protein intake at a moderate level and balanced with other macronutrients.

Carbohydrates

Carbohydrates control insulin, and insulin controls fat storage. All forms of carbohydrates, simple and complex, are eventually converted into glucose (sugar). As we've seen, glucose that is not burned immediately will first be stored as glycogen in muscle and liver cells. Once these sites are full it is converted into fatty acids and

stored as fat or exported from the liver into systemic circulation meaning that blood sugar levels stay higher for longer. If you constantly eat carbohydrates without depleting stored glycogen (during exercise), you will eventually start to put on fat.

In my plans, your carbohydrate intake is strategic, eating higher carbohydrate meals on your workout days to replenish your depleted glycogen stores after intense exercise. Your carb intake will come from quality sources, like fruits and vegetables, rather than processed carbohydrates that are nutrient sparse.

SUPPLEMENTS

I believe that taking any form of pre- or post-workout supplement, such as protein powders, carb drinks, or bars, is completely unnecessary when you are eating a diet that is full of nutritious foods. The supplements industry is a multi-million-dollar one with clever marketing and celebrity sports figures as spokespeople, but studies have shown that these have little to no effect on increasing muscle mass or fat loss.

Follow a nutrient-dense diet and fuel your body with real food. Spend your money wisely and buy some real protein from your local farm or butcher in the form of a nice, juicy steak.

GETTING STARTED

Often, the most difficult part of trying to replace a bad habit with a good one is getting started. Here are three steps that I give every single one of my clients. Try to follow them in order:

1. **Clean out** Throw away all junk food, including pre-made meals, sodas, processed foods, refined sugars, snacks, and alcohol (more on this later). This is rule number one; if you don't have temptations in the house, you're giving yourself the best chance of success. (This one is crucial for me—if I know there is a delicious brownie in the cupboard, it will get eaten!)

2. **Breakfast or dinner?** Choose whether you are going to skip breakfast or dinner, and stick to that decision. It's crucial that your body gets used to one eating pattern. I find skipping breakfast is the most effective method for me, but everyone is different. Your choice should reflect your lifestyle, as discussed in the previous chapter.

3. **Get organized** Pick 5 to 10 meals from the recipe section that you think you will enjoy the most and go and buy the ingredients. Here is a list of essential ingredients every kitchen should have in order to make a variety of tasty, nutritious meals:

   - Sea salt
   - Black pepper
   - Extra virgin olive oil
   - Butter from grass-fed cows
   - Coconut oil
   - Onions
   - Garlic
   - Canned tomatoes
   - Soy sauce (light or dark)
   - Chiles
   - Full-fat Greek yogurt
   - Whole almonds
   - Peanut butter (or any other nut butter, such as cashew, almond, or hazelnut)
   - Fresh ginger
   - Dark chocolate (approx. 70 percent cocoa solids)
   - Lemons/limes
   - Paprika
   - Oregano
   - Rosemary

THE PRINCIPLES

Follow these guiding principles to incorporate the 2MD into your life:

1. **Eat at normal times** Although you're skipping a meal, don't change the times you eat your other two meals. So, if you are planning on skipping breakfast and you normally eat lunch at 1pm and dinner at 8pm, stick to these times.

2. **Stick to two meals every day** While you have specific fat-loss goals, there will be no days off.

3. **No cheating!** Consume only water, black tea or coffee (no milk or sugar), or herbal tea during your fast. Be strategic with caffeine—hold off on your morning coffee until you can't wait any longer. (Caffeine can help to blunt your appetite.) Do not snack during your fast. You can have one snack (pages 132–149) between your two meals, but not during your fasting period.

OBSTACLES

Inevitably, there may be some teething problems when attempting to transform the way you eat. Give your body time to adjust and you will soon reap the rewards. There are three main difficulties that you may experience:

- **Tummy rumbling** Having an empty stomach can initially be a strange sensation. However, it is important to note that your empty stomach rumbling is not an indication of hunger. Your body works very well on routine; the rumbling is your body expecting to digest food at the time you would normally eat. The best way to remedy this is to drink a big glass of cold water, which will quickly alleviate the problem. After a few days following the 2MD the rumbling will disappear.

• **Light-headedness/headaches** This is especially common when first starting fasted exercise, but it can also occur during normal day-to-day activities. It is often caused by one of two things, if not both. The first is dehydration; try drinking a glass of water with a couple of pinches of salt. Salt is an electrolyte, so when it is added to water it dissolves into its component ions. These ions are electrically conductive and help receive and send messages throughout the body, and facilitate cell hydration. You can also add lemon juice to taste if you wish. Or it could just be that your body has gotten so used to being fueled by sugars from food it is struggling to find energy. Stick with it. Once you get through the initial transition stage where your body starts to tap into stored body fat for energy, you won't get headaches or light-headedness. It may take longer for some people than others, depending on previous daily carbohydrate intake.

• **Social difficulties** Perhaps the hardest thing about the 2MD is having to deal with other people's opinions about skipping meals. People can get very defensive, quoting all sorts of statements about how unhealthy it is. My advice to you when confronted with those opinions is to accept that for lots of people food is a very emotional/sensitive subject and it's not worth getting into an argument over. You can try informing them of the benefits of fasting in the most non-aggressive way possible and leave it at that. Let the haters hate and don't allow it to knock your motivation.

WHAT ABOUT ALCOHOL?

Lifestyle can have a big impact on the success of the 2MD, particularly habits many of us have when socializing. Alcohol is clearly relevant here, and some of you may have been thinking about this very point when reading the section on macronutrients (see pages 23–25). It is a very common concern that I get asked about all the time.

First things first—alcohol stops your body from burning fat, so ideally, if you want to get the best possible results from the 2MD, you shouldn't consume any at all. Having said that, you do not have to give up alcohol to get positive results from this plan. (Although if you are skipping dinner you may want to be careful about consuming alcohol late in the day.) You shouldn't have to put your social life on hold to reach your goals; in fact, trying to do this can make it much harder. The more you obsess about your diet and workouts, the more likely you are to mess it up or lose motivation.

Eating and exercising properly aren't the only contributors to a balanced lifestyle; being sociable plays a big role in our general health and well-being. We are naturally creatures of habit, and socializing can be a problem if we let ourselves get into bad habits, but with a little willpower and self-awareness we can very quickly form new patterns of behavior.

The main bad habit around alcohol is the binge-drinking mentality. It took a long time for me to change my behavior, but after five years of horrendous hangovers, wasting money, hurting myself, damaging relationships, and generally feeling terrible, I managed to form new drinking habits. I still drink on occasion, but not in the same way that I used to, and rarely enough to get drunk.

There are lots of reasons why people end up binge drinking, but I think that most people can relate to the following two. Firstly, people often establish regular and excessive drinking patterns without thinking about it. I got into the habit of having a drink in my hand whenever I was out and would feel awkward and strange standing in a bar without one. I also established a routine of drinking quickly without giving it a thought.

The second reason is social insecurity. Alcohol can be a useful social lubricant, especially when meeting new people. Getting drunk rids us of our inhibitions; we stop caring what others think and just want to have fun. We stop judging ourselves and live in the moment.

So what to do? The five simple steps below helped me to change my drinking behavior:

YOU DO NOT HAVE TO GIVE UP ALCOHOL TO GET POSITIVE RESULTS FROM THIS PLAN

1. **Go out intending not to get drunk** If you repeat "I am not going to get drunk" multiple times to yourself, you are far less likely to get drunk.

2. **Give yourself an excuse to say "no" to another drink** Plan a workout with a friend the next morning, make an early-morning commitment, such as a work meeting or exercise class, or just make something up!

3. **Quality over quantity** Find an alcoholic drink that you genuinely enjoy the taste of and spend more money on quality. Sip it slowly, savor the flavors, and enjoy it. This completely changed the way I drink; I learned to appreciate alcohol, rather than using it as a means to an end.

4. **Drink water** Get into the habit of drinking one glass of water for every alcoholic drink. Not only will it sober you up, but you will be so thankful for it the next day! You may

even realize that you don't want alcohol, but just want the feeling of a drink in your hand. I often have soda water and fresh lime juice as a non-alcoholic alternative.

5. **DO NOT drink shots!** This was a game-changer for me. I was able to stay in control just drinking beer or wine, but as soon as shots entered the equation that was the end of it.

Develop a "sober confidence"

Being able to go out and remain sober or just have a couple of drinks is an incredible skill. It will help you get in great shape and develop a natural confidence—not a false sense of confidence dependent on alcohol. Approach this in the same way you would learn to play the piano or acquire any new skill; you are trying to form new neural pathways in the brain, which takes practice and patience. This is the basis for changing your behaviors and habits.

It may be difficult to begin with, and you may certainly feel uncomfortable at first. But keep practicing and it will become easier. Bear in mind that the first interactions of an evening out will be the hardest, but eventually you will relax and have fun. I find it helps to spend time with a non-drinking friend at the start of the evening.

Slowly but surely you will realize that you don't need alcohol to enjoy yourself. Drinking less also helps you to develop great social skills and enables you to stay composed and in control. You will reach a state in which you feel at ease without being drunk; nothing holds you back, you feel confident and in the moment.

Long-established negative behaviors won't fix themselves overnight, but small changes like these over a long period can have a profound effect on the rest of your life, as well as aiding your health and fitness goals.

RECIPES

Once you have decided which meal you want to skip, follow the respective meal plan for either Breakfast and Lunch (pages 32–33) or Lunch and Dinner (pages 34–35). It is important to try to stick to the workout/rest day schedule, but the exact dishes are not set in stone as long as you follow the guidelines below:

Training Days: Eat one meal from the Higher Carb chapter (pages 36–71) and one from the Lower Carb chapter (pages 72–131), plus one snack between those meals if you wish (pages 132–149). Snacks are completely optional. If you want to enjoy a dessert (pages 150–167), then you can do so on two training days per week instead of eating a snack that day.

You can do the workouts at any time of time of day, but try to train fasted first thing in the morning if you can.

Rest Days: Eat two meals from the Lower Carb chapter (pages 72–131) and one snack between those meals if you wish (pages 132–149).

During your fasted period, just consume water (still or sparkling), black coffee or tea, or any kind of tea, such as green or mint tea.

MEAL PLANS
Breakfast and Lunch

	Monday R1 (pp.180–182)	Tuesday HIIT 1 (pp.186–187)	Wednesday REST	Thursday HIIT 1 (pp.186–187)	Friday REST	Saturday R1 (pp.180–182)	Sunday REST
Breakfast	Mushrooms and Bacon on Toast (p.47)	Baked Kale and Eggs (p.81)	Mushroom Omelet (p.74)	Shakshuka (p.120)	Smoked Salmon Mini Frittatas (p.78)	Classic Bacon and Poached Egg (p.77)	Egg Guacamole Goodness Bowl (p.82)
Snack	Tuna Guacamole (p.134)	None	Peanut Butter and Banana on Rye (p.140)	Homemade Beet Hummus and Carrot Sticks (p.143)	Eggplant Dip (p.137)	None	Sliced Tomato and Mozzarella (p.147)
Lunch	Shrimp salad in a Jar (p.84)	Tuna Casserole (p.55) ———— Two-ingredient Chocolate Mousse (p.152)	Chicken Breast with Sun-dried Tomato Pesto Zucchini Noodles (p.124)	Mexican Sweet Potato Skins with Guacamole (p.48)	Pork Tenderloin with Peanut Butter Satay and an Asian Slaw (p.131)	Soy and Honey-glazed Chicken with Coconut Rice (p.41) ———— Frozen Berry Smoothie Bowl (p.156)	Seared Tuna and Crunchy Asian Asparagus Salad (p.103)

	Monday R2 (p.183–185)	Tuesday HIIT 2 (p.188–189)	Wednesday REST	Thursday HIIT 2 (p.188–189)	Friday REST	Saturday R2 (p.183–185)	Sunday REST
Breakfast	Salmon Goodness Bowl (p.45)	Mushrooms and Bacon on Toast (p.47)	Smoked Salmon Mini Frittatas (p.78)	Round Steak with an Herb vinaigrette and Swiss Chard (p.127)	Egg Guacamole Goodness Bowl (p.82)	Baked Kale and Eggs (p.81)	Shakshuka (p.120)
Snack	Avocado and Feta on Sourdough (p.147)	Deviled Eggs (p.141)	Cottage Cheese and Tomato Ham Wraps (p.148)	None	Roasted Spiced Chickpeas (p.144)	None	Smoky Chicken Skewers (p.144)
Lunch	Eggplant Mini Pizzas (p.92)	Thai Green Chicken Curry (p.99)	Chicken with Creamy Bacon and Mushroom Sauce (p.91)	Spiced Rice (p.62) ———— Two-ingredient Peanut Butter Fudge (p.155)	Baked Mackerel and Garlic Pesto (p.118)	Sweet Potato, Pine Nut, and Feta Salad (p.57) ———— Banana Chocolate Pancakes (p.158)	Beef Stroganoff (p.94)

	Monday R1 (pp.180–182)	Tuesday HIIT 1 (pp.186–187)	Wednesday REST	Thursday HIIT 1 (pp.186–187)	Friday REST	Saturday R1 (pp.180–182)	Sunday REST
Breakfast	Smoked Salmon Mini Frittatas (p.78)	Mexican Cheese Steak Melt (p.42)	Egg Guacamole Goodness Bowl (p.82)	Classic Bacon and Poached Egg (p.77)	Goat Cheese and Tomato Pesto Frittata (p.83)	Baked Kale and Eggs (p.81)	Mushroom Omelet (p.74)
Snack	Smoky Chicken Skewers (p.144)	Feta and Sun-dried Tomato Dip (p.134)	Chile-roasted Almonds (p.148)	None	Apple with Almond Butter (p.140)	None	Tuna Guacamole (p.134)
Lunch	Creamy Mushroom and Parmesan Risotto (p.52)	Sea Bass with Sauce Vierge (p.128)	Scallops with Pancetta and Spinach (p.117)	Mozzarella Chicken (p.58) —— Raw Caramel Apple Cookies (p.159)	Pork Tenderloin with Peanut Butter Satay and an Asian Slaw (p.131)	Fish Casserole with Butternut Squash (p.65) —— Raw Chocolate Brownie (p.165)	Italian Lamb Chops (p.109)

	Monday R2 (pp.183–185)	Tuesday HIIT 2 (pp.188–189)	Wednesday REST	Thursday HIIT 2 (pp.188–189)	Friday REST	Saturday R2 (pp.183–185)	Sunday REST
Breakfast	Mushrooms and Bacon on Toast (p.47)	Egg Guacamole Goodness Bowl (p.82)	Smoked Salmon Mini Frittatas (p.78)	Mushroom Omelet (p.74)	Goat Cheese and Tomato Pesto Fritatta (p.83)	Breakfast Burritos (p.46)	Shakshuka (p.120)
Snack	None	Cottage Cheese and Tomato Ham Wraps (p.148)	Peanut Butter and Banana on Rye (p.140)	Smoked Mackerel Pâté (p.138)	Sliced Tomato and Mozzarella (p.147)	None	Homemade Beet Hummus and Carrot Sticks (p.143)
Lunch	Blue-cheese-stuffed Portobello Mushrooms (p.100) —— Seasonal Berries with Coconut Cream (p.164)	Honey-glazed Sesame Beef with Soba Noodles (p.61)	One-pan Chorizo with Beans (p.113)	Baked Tomato Gnocchi (p.71)	Chile-covered Salmon with Spinach (p.110)	Shrimp and Tomato Curry (p.104) —— Grilled Fruit with Honey and Ricotta (p.162)	Eggplant Parmigiana with Mediterranean Salad (p.114)

Lunch and Dinner

	Monday R1 (pp.180–182)	Tuesday HIIT 1 (pp.186–187)	Wednesday REST	Thursday HIIT 1 (pp.186–187)	Friday REST	Saturday R1 (pp.180–182)	Sunday REST
Lunch	Creamy Cashew Soba Noodles (p.38)	Baked Beet, Walnut, and Goat Cheese Salad (p.96)	Grilled Zucchini Salad with Anchovies and Capers (p.87)	Mushroom Omelet (p.74)	Shrimp salad in a Jar (p.84)	Classic Bacon and Poached Egg (p.77)	Pork Tenderloin with Creamy Goat Cheese Sauce (p.88)
Snack	Tuna Guacamole (p.134)	Smoked Mackerel Pâté (p.138)	Peanut Butter and Banana on Rye (p.140)	None	Eggplant Dip (p.137)	None	Peanut Butter and Banana on Rye (p.140)
Dinner	Eggplant Parmigiana with Mediterranean Salad (p.114)	Spiced Rice (p.62)	Chicken Breast with Sun-dried Tomato Pesto Zucchini Noodles (p.124)	Mexican Sweet Potato Skins with Guacamole (p.48) ___ Seasonal Berries with Coconut Cream (p.164)	Pork Tenderloin with Peanut Satay and an Asian Slaw (p.131)	Soy and Honey-glazed Chicken with Coconut Rice (p.41) ___ Raw Chocolate Macadamia Bark (p.161)	Seared Tuna and Crunchy Asian Asparagus Salad (p.103)

	Monday R2 (pp.183–185)	Tuesday HIIT 2 (pp.188–189)	Wednesday REST	Thursday HIIT 2 (pp.188–89)	Friday REST	Saturday R2 (pp.183–185)	Sunday REST
Lunch	Salmon Goodness Bowl (p.45)	Creamy Goat Cheese Spaghetti with Spinach, Bacon, and Mushrooms (p.51)	Smoked Salmon Mini Frittatas (p.78)	Round Steak with an Herb vinaigrette and Swiss Chard (p.127)	Egg Guacamole Goodness Bowl (p.82)	Baked Kale and Eggs (p.81)	Baked Beet, Walnut, and Goat Cheese Salad (p.96)
Snack	Avocado and Feta on Sourdough (p.147)	Deviled Eggs (p.141)	Cottage Cheese and Tomato Ham Wraps (p.148)	None	Roasted Spiced Chickpeas (p.144)	None	Eggplant Dip (p.137)
Dinner	Eggplant Mini Pizzas (p.92)	Thai Green Chicken Curry (p.99)	Chicken with Creamy Bacon and Mushroom Sauce (p.91)	Spiced Rice (p.62) ___ Raw Chocolate Brownie (p.165)	Baked Mackerel and Garlic Pesto (p.118)	Sweet Potato, Pine Nut, and Feta Salad (p.57) ___ Chocolate Banana Milkshake (p.167)	Beef Stroganoff (p.94)

	Monday R1 (pp.180–182)	Tuesday HIIT 1 (pp.186–187)	Wednesday REST	Thursday HIIT 1 (pp.186–187)	Friday REST	Saturday R1 (pp.180–182)	Sunday REST
Lunch	Chile-covered Salmon with Spinach (p.110)	Mexican Cheese Steak Melt (p.42)	Chicken Breast with a Lemon Yogurt Sauce (p.107)	Tuna Lettuce Cups (p.106)	Goat Cheese and Tomato Pesto Frittata (p.83)	Creamed Swiss Chard with Pine Nuts (p.121)	Eggplant Parmigiana Mediterranean Salad (p.114)
Snack	Smoky Chicken Skewers (p.144)	Feta and Sun-dried Tomato Dip (p.134)	Chile-roasted Almonds (p.148)	None	Apple with Almond Butter (p.140)	None	Tuna Guacamole (p.134)
Dinner	Creamy Mushroom and Parmesan Risotto (p.52)	Sea Bass with Sauce Vierge (p.128)	Scallops with Pancetta and Spinach (p.117)	Mozzarella Chicken with (p.58) ⎯⎯⎯ Raw Caramel Apple Cookies (p.159)	Pork Tenderloin with Peanut Butter Satay and an Asian Slaw (131)	Fish Casserole with Butternut Squash (p.65) ⎯⎯⎯ Two-ingredient Peanut Butter Fudge (p.155)	Italian Lamb Chops (p.109)

	Monday R2 (pp.183–185)	Tuesday HIIT 2 (pp.188–189)	Wednesday REST	Thursday HIIT 2 (pp.188–189)	Friday REST	Saturday R2 (pp.183–185)	Sunday REST
Lunch	Tomato Pesto Quinoa with Spinach (p.69)	Baked Mackerel and Garlic Pesto (p.118)	Trout with Bacon and Peas (p.123)	Teriyaki Turkey Burgers (p.95)	Shrimp salad in a Jar (p.84)	Breakfast Burritos (p.46)	Shakshuka (p.120)
Snack	Chile-roasted Almonds (p.148)	None	Peanut Butter and Banana on Rye (p.140)	Smoked Mackerel Pâté (p.138)	Sliced Tomato and Mozzarella (p.147)	None	Homemade Beet Hummus and Carrot Sticks (p.143)
Dinner	Blue-cheese-stuffed Portobello Mushrooms (p.100)	Avocado Pesto Spaghetti (p.54) ⎯⎯⎯ Grilled Fruit with Honey and Ricotta (p.162)	One-pan Chorizo with Beans (p.113)	Baked Tomato Gnocchi (p.71)	Chile-covered Salmon with Spinach (p.110)	Shrimp and Tomato Curry (p.104) ⎯⎯⎯ Banana and Chocolate Pancakes (p.158)	Pork Tenderloin with Creamy Goat Cheese Sauce (p.88)

HIGHER CARB RECIPES

This is not an extremely low-carb diet. Your carbohydrate intake is strategic to on training days eat one of your two meals from this chapter and the other from the lower carb one (pages 72–131).

Eating in this way means that you will use carbohydrates to create lean muscle mass rather than fat storage. But it's important that your carbohydrate intake comes from quality sources like fruits and vegetables.

Buckwheat has a surprisingly high protein content and is a good-quality carbohydrate source. Despite the name, buckwheat is not a form of wheat. In fact, it is closely related to sorrel, knotweed, and rhubarb. So these noodles can be enjoyed with none of the negative side effects that some people can get from eating grains.

CREAMY CASHEW SOBA (BUCKWHEAT) NOODLES

SERVES: 2
PREP: 7 MINUTES
COOKING: 5 MINUTES

FOR THE NOODLES
5½ ounces soba noodles
2 large carrots, grated
1½ cups red cabbage, thinly sliced
2 scallions, very finely sliced
a handful of mint, finely chopped
a handful of roasted cashews
a handful of cilantro, finely chopped, plus extra to garnish

FOR THE DRESSING
2 tablespoons cashew butter
1 tablespoon fresh ginger, peeled and grated
1 garlic clove
2 tablespoons lime juice
2 tablespoons toasted sesame oil
1 tablespoon rice vinegar
2 tablespoons dark soy sauce
salt and freshly ground black pepper

Cook the noodles according to the package instructions, rinse with cold water, and set aside.

Meanwhile, combine all the dressing ingredients together in a food processor.

Mix everything together in a big bowl and serve, topped with fresh cilantro.

Coconut rice is one of those dishes I discovered while traveling through Thailand and couldn't wait to recreate once I got home. The rice is so simple and tastes amazing, pairing beautifully with the soy and honey chicken.

SOY AND HONEY-GLAZED CHICKEN WITH COCONUT RICE

SERVES: 2
PREP: 5 MINUTES
COOKING: 30 MINUTES

2 tablespoons honey
2 tablespoons dark soy sauce
10½ ounces boneless chicken thighs, skin on
½ cup brown rice
½ cup unsweetened coconut milk
salt
1 tablespoon toasted sesame oil
2 heads bok choy, chopped
1 tablespoon coconut oil
1 tablespoon black sesame seeds
a handful of cilantro leaves
1 tablespoon pumpkin seeds, chopped

In a bowl, mix together the honey and soy sauce. Add the chicken thighs and mix until completely coated in the marinade. Place the chicken into a deep, heavy-bottomed saucepan. Cook over medium heat for about 20 minutes until the chicken is cooked through and the honey and soy coating has thickened to a glossy glaze.

Meanwhile, add the rice, coconut milk, ¼ cup water, and a pinch of salt to a separate pan and bring to a boil. Once the water is boiling, reduce the heat and simmer the rice, covered, for about 30 minutes until tender.

Heat the sesame oil in a large frying pan over medium heat. Add the bok choy and cook for 3 to 5 minutes.

Fluff the cooked rice with a fork, then stir in the coconut oil, sesame seeds, and cilantro. Sprinkle with the chopped pumpkin seeds. To serve, spoon the rice onto plates and top with the chicken. Place the bok choy on the side.

You can't really beat the combination of cheese, steak, avocado, tomatoes, and good sourdough bread, especially if the cheese happens to be melted. If you start losing motivation halfway through a workout, just picture this melt as your well-deserved reward, and I guarantee it will get you moving again. Grass-fed beef has more nutrients than corn fed, like the B-vitamins thiamin and riboflavin, which help you to extract energy from food.

MEXICAN CHEESE STEAK MELT

SERVES: 1
PREP: 5 MINUTES
COOKING: 15 MINUTES

7 ounces grass-fed steak
salt and freshly ground black pepper
½ red onion, diced
1 medium tomato, diced
½ avocado
1 tablespoon lime juice
4 slices of Cheddar cheese
2 slices of sourdough bread, buttered on both sides
pat of grass-fed butter

Sprinkle the steak with salt and pepper, then sear it over high heat for 2 minutes on each side, flipping every minute (for rare). Set aside.

Cook the onion with the tomato for 5 to 10 minutes until the onion is translucent and soft. Mash the avocado with salt, pepper, and the lime juice.

Layer the steak, avocado and tomato mixture, and Cheddar on a slice of buttered sourdough. Top with the other slice.

Melt the butter in a frying pan over high heat. Place the sandwich in the pan and put a baking sheet, plate, or anything flat on top of the sandwich and weigh it down with a few cans. Cook the sandwich for 2 minutes on each side, being very careful when you flip it.

These simple bowls are full of goodness. Kale is packed with vitamin K, iron, and folate, which help to build strong bones and are important for healthy red blood cells. Butternut squash contains lots of vitamin B6, which is crucial for the immune system and salmon is a source of omega-3 fatty acids, which are great for your skin, brain function, and cardiovascular health. Cooking kale in this way helps retain the nutrients and also means it tastes great!

SALMON GOODNESS BOWL

SERVES: 1
PREP: 5 MINUTES
COOKING: 20 MINUTES

1 salmon fillet, skin on
salt and freshly ground black pepper
3 tablespoons grass-fed butter
3 thin slices of lemon
7 ounces butternut squash, peeled and cut into
   1-inch cubes (about 1½ cups)
7 ounces kale
¾ cup edamame beans, shelled and cooked

Preheat the oven to 400°F.

Season the salmon with salt and pepper, then dot 1 tablespoon of the butter evenly over the fish, layering the lemon slices on top. Wrap it all up in foil, skin-side down. Roast for 20 minutes.

Meanwhile, melt 1 tablespoon of butter in a large frying pan and cook the butternut squash for 10 to 15 minutes until tender.

Five minutes before the salmon is ready, melt the remaining tablespoon of butter in a frying pan over high heat and cook the kale for 5 minutes, adding plenty of salt, so it gets crispy.

Place all the ingredients, including the edamame beans, in a bowl and serve with the salmon on top.

These breakfast burritos are decadently delicious while also filling you up with lots of nutrients. Avocado is one of my favorite foods, packed full of vitamins and also a good source of potassium. This dish is guaranteed to fill even the most bottomless stomachs. And the good news is: breakfast-like meals can be enjoyed at any time of the day.

BREAKFAST BURRITOS

SERVES: 1
PREP: 2 MINUTES
COOKING: 10 MINUTES

1 tablespoon grass-fed butter
7 ounces grass-fed steak
salt and freshly ground black pepper
2 large eggs, free range and preferably organic
1 avocado, peeled and pitted
2 whole-grain burrito wraps
4 cherry tomatoes, diced

Heat the butter in a pan and season the steak with lots of salt and pepper. Cook the steak over high heat for 2 minutes on each side (for rare).

Meanwhile, scramble the eggs in a little butter. Mash the avocado. Place the burritos on a cutting board or large plate, slice the steak into thin strips, and layer the burritos with the steak, avocado, tomatoes, and egg. Wrap up and enjoy!

Sometimes the simplest things taste the best. Creamy mushrooms, bacon, and toasted rye bread are a delicious combination. For most of my life I didn't like mushrooms, but then I decided to approach them with an open mind and now I love them.

MUSHROOMS AND BACON ON TOAST

SERVES: 1
PREP: 2 MINUTES
COOKING: 10 MINUTES

2 tablespoons grass-fed butter
2 slices of prosciutto
1 cup mixed mushrooms, coarsely chopped
1 garlic clove, crushed
1 tablespoon crème fraîche
1 large slice of rye bread
salt and freshly ground black pepper
a handful of flat-leaf parsley, finely chopped

Melt half the butter a large frying pan. Cook the prosciutto for about 2 minutes on each side until golden and crisp. Break into large pieces and set aside on some paper towels.

Add the remaining butter to the pan, followed by the mushrooms. Cook for 2 minutes, then add the garlic and crème fraîche. Cook for another 3 to 5 minutes, until the mushrooms are soft and lightly coated in the crème fraîche.

Meanwhile, toast the rye bread in a toaster or under the broiler.

Season the mushrooms with salt and pepper and stir in a little of the parsley. Pile up on the rye toast and top with the prosciutto and the remaining parsley.

Sweet potatoes are the perfect post-workout food. Not only are they a good source of carbohydrates to replenish glycogen stores after exercise, they also contain high amounts of vitamin A, which helps your immune system to fight off infections as well as contributing to healthy skin.

MEXICAN SWEET POTATO SKINS WITH GUACAMOLE

SERVES: 1
PREP: 10 MINUTES
COOKING: 45 MINUTES

1 sweet potato
1 tablespoon extra virgin olive oil
1 large avocado, peeled and pitted
juice of 1 lime, plus extra wedges to serve
1 red chile, seeded and finely chopped
2 tomatoes, diced
a handful of cilantro, leaves coarsely chopped
1 small red onion, finely chopped
1 cup canned kidney beans, drained and rinsed

Preheat the oven to 425°F.

Coat the sweet potato with the oil, then roast for 45 minutes or until tender all the way through.

Meanwhile, mash the avocado with the lime juice in a small bowl, then stir in the chile, tomatoes, cilantro, and onion.

Cut the sweet potato in half and top with the beans and guacamole. Serve with lime wedges.

This is one of those dishes that you just look at and feel sure that you shouldn't be eating it. It seems to tick too many naughty boxes to be good for you. Well, good news: following a workout, this is a well-deserved treat to be enjoyed without a smidgen of guilt. The carbohydrates in the spaghetti will be redirected to your muscles to aid recovery and help promote lean muscle growth.

CREAMY GOAT CHEESE SPAGHETTI WITH SPINACH, BACON, AND MUSHROOMS

SERVES: 1
PREP: 5 MINUTES
COOKING: 15 MINUTES

3½ ounces spaghetti
2 tablespoons olive oil
½ onion, diced
2 slices of thick-cut bacon, chopped
¼ cup hot vegetable stock
¾ cup frozen peas
2 to 3 tablespoons goat cheese
1½ cups spinach
salt and freshly ground black pepper

Cook the pasta according to the package instructions.

Meanwhile, heat the oil in a large frying pan, then add the onion and cook for 3 minutes until starting to soften. Add the bacon, cook for another 5 minutes, then pour in the stock and bring to a boil. Simmer for a few minutes until the liquid has reduced slightly.

Stir in the peas, followed by the goat cheese, until the cheese has melted and the peas are defrosted. Quickly stir through the spinach to wilt. Drain the pasta and mix with the sauce. Season with salt and black pepper to taste.

There is nothing more satisfying than a creamy Italian risotto; the mushrooms and Parmesan pair perfectly with the tasty rice. Risotto dishes are gratifyingly easy to get right, and you are rewarded with a fantastically tasty dish in no time.

CREAMY MUSHROOM AND PARMESAN RISOTTO

SERVES: 2
PREP: 5 MINUTES
COOKING: 30 TO 35 MINUTES

2 tablespoons olive oil
1 onion, chopped
1 garlic clove, crushed
9 ounces crimini mushrooms, sliced (about 3 cups)
salt and freshly ground black pepper
1½ cups risotto rice, such as arborio or carnaroli
¾ cup white wine
1½ cups hot chicken stock
¾ cup freshly grated Parmesan cheese, plus extra to serve
a handful of flat-leaf parsley, chopped

Heat the oil in a deep frying pan over medium heat. Add the onion and garlic and cook for 5 minutes until soft. Stir in the mushrooms, season with salt and pepper, and cook for another 5 to 7 minutes.

Add the rice and cook for 2 to 3 minutes until the edges become translucent. Do not let the rice brown. Then pour in the wine and cook until it has completely evaporated.

Pour in about one-quarter of the stock and simmer slowly, stirring constantly. Once the rice has absorbed all the liquid, add another quarter of the stock, simmer, and stir again. Repeat this process until all the stock has been absorbed and the rice is almost cooked, stirring constantly for about 20 minutes. It should have the consistency of oatmeal.

Add the Parmesan and parsley and stir to combine. Let rest for 5 minutes before serving in bowls topped with extra Parmesan and a twist of black pepper.

Avocados are packed full of nutrients. They contain high amounts of vitamins B5, B6, C, E, and K, which all have a role in supporting the proper functioning of the immune system. They are also high in monounsaturated fat which maintains levels of good (HDL) cholesterol while reducing levels of bad (LDL) cholesterol.

AVOCADO PESTO SPAGHETTI

SERVES: 2
PREP: 5 MINUTES
COOKING: 12 MINUTES

2 ounces pancetta
salt
7 ounces spaghetti
2 handfuls of Parmesan cheese, freshly grated
2 handfuls of basil, plus extra to garnish (optional)
2 handfuls of pine nuts
1 avocado, peeled, pitted, and coarsely chopped
juice of ½ lemon
2 tablespoons grass-fed butter
2 garlic cloves, minced

Bring a large saucepan of water to a boil. Finely dice the pancetta, having first removed any rind.

Add 1 teaspoon of salt to the boiling water, add the spaghetti, and when the water comes back to a boil, cook on a rolling boil, covered, for 10 minutes or until al dente.

Meanwhile, process the Parmesan, basil, pine nuts, avocado, and lemon juice together in a blender or food processor.

Melt the butter in a large, deep frying pan over medium heat, then add the garlic and pancetta. Cook for 5 minutes, stirring constantly, then reduce the heat to low.

When the pasta is ready, lift it from the water using a spaghetti fork or tongs and add it to the frying pan. Add the avocado pesto and mix it all together.

Serve in bowls, garnished with basil, if you wish.

This is a twist on the traditional tuna casserole, using quinoa instead of pasta. Quinoa is much higher in nutrients than pasta and is also a very good source of calcium, magnesium, and manganese. Super simple and super tasty!

TUNA CASSEROLE

SERVES: 1
PREP: 5 MINUTES
COOKING: 25 MINUTES

5½ ounces canned tuna
¾ cup Greek yogurt
3 tablespoons chicken stock
1 cup quinoa, cooked
¼ cup red onion, diced
½ cup broccoli, coarsely chopped
1 tablespoon crushed garlic
½ teaspoon ground cumin
½ teaspoon oregano
salt and freshly ground black pepper
a handful of freshly grated Parmesan cheese

Preheat the oven to 400°F.

Mix all the ingredients, except the Parmesan, in a bowl.

Transfer to a baking dish. Scatter the Parmesan on top and bake for 20 minutes. Serve with your choice of leafy greens.

Swap your standard potato salad for this sweet potato version. Sweet potato has a lower glycemic index than normal potatoes. (The glycemic index rates foods on how much, and how quickly they raise your blood sugar levels.) Meaning sweet potato won't cause as high a spike in blood sugar compared to regular potatoes, further assisting fat burning.

SWEET POTATO, PINE NUT, AND FETA SALAD

SERVES: 2
PREP: 10 MINUTES
COOKING: 35 MINUTES

1 pound sweet potatoes, peeled and cut into large chunks
1 tablespoon extra virgin olive oil
salt and freshly ground black pepper
½ cup feta cheese, roughly crumbled
¼ cup pine nuts, toasted

FOR THE DRESSING
2 scallions, finely chopped
a handful of flat-leaf parsley, chopped
2 tablespoons extra virgin olive oil
1 tablespoon honey
¼ cup white wine vinegar

Preheat the oven to 400°F.

Toss the sweet potatoes with the oil and some salt and pepper. Spread on a foil-lined baking sheet and roast for 30 to 35 minutes until tender. Let cool to room temperature.

Whisk all the dressing ingredients together with a little more salt and pepper. Pile the potatoes onto a serving plate and drizzle with the dressing. Scatter with the feta and pine nuts, and gently toss with your hands so you don't break up the sweet potato chunks.

This is a delicious way of cooking chicken, keeping it nice and moist in the rich tomato sauce. The creamy lima bean mash complements the chicken perfectly, absorbing all the lovely tomato sauce. Lima beans are a good source of protein and fiber and therefore have a considerably lower glycemic-index score than potatoes, which means they won't affect your blood-sugar levels in the same way.

MOZZARELLA CHICKEN

SERVES: 2
PREP: 5 MINUTES
COOKING: 20 MINUTES

2 chicken breasts, skin on
salt and black pepper
extra virgin olive oil
½ medium onion, thinly sliced
2 garlic cloves, crushed
1 x 14-ounce can chopped
  tomatoes
3 tablespoons tomato sauce
1 tablespoon dried oregano
½ cup pitted green or black
  olives, coarsely chopped
4½-ounce mozzarella ball, sliced

FOR THE LIMA BEAN MASH
1 tablespoon grass-fed butter
½ medium onion, finely
  chopped
1 garlic clove, crushed
1 x 14-ounce can lima beans,
  drained and rinsed
2 tablespoons heavy cream or
  crème fraîche

Preheat the oven to 400°F. Season the chicken with salt and pepper.

Heat 2 tablespoons of oil in a large frying pan over high heat. Sear the chicken for 3 minutes on each side or until lightly browned. Transfer to a plate. Reduce the heat, add a little more oil, and cook the onion for 4 to 5 minutes, stirring until softened and lightly browned. Add the garlic and cook for a few seconds. Pour in the tomatoes, then stir in the tomato sauce, oregano, olives, and a splash of cold water. Bring to a boil and cook for 5 minutes, stirring regularly. Reduce the heat to a simmer and add the chicken. Cook for 10 minutes, stirring occasionally, until the chicken is tender and cooked through. Season to taste.

Transfer to a baking dish. Top the chicken with the mozzarella and sprinkle with ground black pepper. Bake for 8 to 10 minutes.

Meanwhile, make the mash: Heat the butter in a saucepan over medium heat. Add the onion and cook for 3 minutes. Add the garlic and cook for another minute. Add the lima beans and cook for 5 minutes until soft. Mash using a potato masher, adding the cream as you do so. Serve alongside the chicken.

If you are craving something with an Asian twist, this is your dish—a wonderfully balanced noodle recipe with steak and vegetables and a killer dressing. Soba noodles are a gluten-free alternative to traditional noodles, as they are made out of buckwheat, which is closer to rhubarb than it is to wheat. They are also a good source of thiamine (also known as vitamin B1), which is essential for helping the body turn food into energy, and are high in protein and soluble fiber.

HONEY-GLAZED SESAME BEEF WITH SOBA NOODLES

SERVES: 1
PREP: 7 MINUTES
COOKING: 20 MINUTES

FOR THE SAUCE
3 tablespoons beef stock
1 tablespoon honey
2 tablespoons soy sauce
1¼-inch piece of fresh ginger, peeled and minced
1 tablespoon toasted sesame oil
1 garlic clove, crushed
1 tablespoon white rice vinegar

FOR THE BEEF AND NOODLES
1 tablespoon toasted sesame oil
7 ounces grass-fed round steak, cut into ¾-inch thick slices
1 red bell pepper, thinly sliced
1¼ cups broccoli, cut into small florets
3½ ounces soba noodles
2 scallions, thinly sliced, to serve and 1 tablespoon white sesame seeds, to garnish

Start by making the sauce: Whisk all the ingredients together.

Heat a wok over medium–high heat with the sesame oil. Add the steak and cook for 3 to 4 minutes. Add the bell pepper and broccoli. Cook together, stirring occasionally, for another 5 minutes.

Cook the noodles in a pan of boiling water for 5 minutes. Drain, rinse under cold water, and set aside.

Reduce the heat under the steak and add the sauce, stirring and shaking the wok for 2 minutes.

Garnish with the scallions and sesame seeds.

This simple dish packs a punch and can be made in only 15 minutes! The carbohydrates in the rice will help you to refuel your muscles after a tough training session, making this an ideal post-workout meal.

SPICED RICE

SERVES: 1
PREP: 5 MINUTES
COOKING: 15 MINUTES

1 cup vegetable stock
2 tablespoons Thai red curry paste
1 red chile, seeded and chopped
½ cup basmati rice
1 tablespoon grass-fed butter
1 medium carrot, peeled and grated
¾ cup edamame beans
2 large eggs, free-range and preferably organic, lightly beaten
salt and freshly ground black pepper

Pour the vegetable stock into a saucepan, then add the red curry paste, chile, and rice. Bring to a boil, cover with a lid, and simmer for 10 minutes until most of the liquid has been absorbed.

Melt the butter in a frying pan, then add the rice together with the carrot and edamame beans. Stir regularly until the rice is moist but no longer wet, then add the beaten eggs. Season with salt and pepper.

Cook, without stirring, for a few minutes, then stir gently to break the mixture up. Continue for a couple of minutes until the egg is lightly cooked and visible in patches through the rice.

This is my dad's recipe and our whole family can't get enough of it! With a creamy filling and a cheesy butternut squash topping, this pie is jam-packed with colors, flavors, and nutrients from the fish, eggs, and vegetables. Using squash and sweet potatoes instead of regular potatoes helps keep your blood-sugar levels more stable.

FISH CASSEROLE WITH BUTTERNUT SQUASH TOPPING

SERVES: 4
PREP: 7 MINUTES
COOKING: 35 MINUTES

1 pound sweet potatoes, peeled and cut into 1¼-inch cubes
1 pound butternut squash, peeled and cut into 1¼-inch cubes
1 tablespoon grass-fed butter
4 scallions
1 medium carrot, diced
1 cup heavy cream
1 teaspoon Dijon or English mustard
juice of ½ lemon
1-ounce package or small bunch of chives, finely chopped
2 handfuls of freshly grated Cheddar cheese
14 ounces fish, one or a mixture of the following: cod, smoked haddock, salmon, and shrimp
3 hard-boiled eggs, free-range and preferably organic, chopped
a handful of frozen peas, plus extra to serve

Preheat the oven to 350°F.

Boil the sweet potatoes and butternut squash for 10 minutes until soft. Mash together with half of the butter and set aside.

Heat the remaining butter in a frying pan over medium–high heat. Cook the scallions and carrots for about 5 minutes until soft, then add the cream, mustard, lemon juice, and chives, and gradually add half the cheese until it melts.

Place the fish in a baking dish and sprinkle the hard-boiled eggs all over the top. Pour the cheese sauce on top and add the peas. Layer the potato and butternut squash mash all over the fish and scatter the remaining cheese over the top.

Cook for 25 minutes. Serve with extra peas.

This simple dish works to bring out the flavor in mackerel, a highly nutritious oily fish and one of the best sources of omega-3 fatty acids and vitamin D, which helps the optimal function of the immune system as well as bone development. Mackerel is sustainable when compared to other fish, and you can normally find it very fresh.

MACKEREL WITH CHICKPEAS AND A BASIL AND LEMON DRESSING

SERVES: 1
PREP: 5 MINUTES
COOKING: 10 MINUTES

2 tablespoons olive oil
1 x 14-ounce can chickpeas, drained and rinsed
¼ cup vegetable stock
5 cherry tomatoes, halved
1 to 2 mackerel fillets (depending on size), skin on
salt and freshly ground pepper

FOR THE DRESSING
2 tablespoons extra virgin olive oil
1 large bunch basil, coarsely chopped
1 bunch scallions, sliced
1 large garlic clove, crushed
juice of 1 lemon

Heat 1 tablespoon of oil in a large saucepan. Add the chickpeas and lightly crush them using a potato masher. Add the stock and tomatoes, simmer for 3 to 4 minutes, or until the liquid is absorbed, then set aside to cool slightly.

Combine all the dressing ingredients together in a food processor and then pour over the chickpeas.

Meanwhile, heat the remaining oil in a large, nonstick frying pan over medium heat. Season the fish all over and cook for 3 minutes on each side, starting on the skin side.

Serve the mackerel on top of the dressed chickpeas.

Quinoa is one of the few plant-based foods that provides all nine essential amino acids. It also contains iron, B vitamins, magnesium, phosphorus, potassium, calcium, vitamin E, and fiber. Try it with a homemade tomato pesto to pack it full of flavor as well as nutrients!

TOMATO PESTO QUINOA WITH SPINACH

SERVES: 1
PREP: 10 MINUTES
COOKING: 8 MINUTES

¾ cup multicolored quinoa
7 ounces baby spinach
salt
a handful of freshly grated Parmesan cheese (optional), plus extra to serve

FOR THE PESTO
a handful of sun-dried tomatoes
a handful of basil, plus extra to serve (optional)
a handful of freshly grated Parmesan cheese
a handful of pine nuts
juice of ½ lemon
freshly ground black pepper

Cook the quinoa according to the package instructions (I use chicken stock instead of water for extra flavor).

While the quinoa is cooking, combine all the pesto ingredients together in a food processor or blender.

When the quinoa is cooked, increase the heat to medium then add the spinach, pesto, salt, and Parmesan. Stir to combine and heat until the spinach has wilted and the pesto is evenly spread.

Serve immediately with extra Parmesan and garnish with basil, if you wish.

This is one of my guilty pleasures and makes for a great meal on a workout day. It's a tasty dish with a range of different textures and flavors to enjoy, from the crunchy cheese on top to the al dente gnocchi and its delicious tomato sauce.

BAKED TOMATO GNOCCHI

SERVES: 4
PREP: 5 MINUTES
COOKING: 25 MINUTES

1 tablespoon extra virgin olive oil
1 onion, finely chopped
1 red bell pepper, finely chopped
1 garlic clove, finely chopped
1 x 14-ounce can chopped tomatoes
18 ounces gnocchi
a handful of basil, coarsely chopped
4½ ounces mozzarella ball, drained and torn into chunks

Preheat the broiler to high.

Heat the oil in a large frying pan, then soften the onion and bell pepper for 5 minutes. Stir in the garlic and cook for 1 minute, then pour in the tomatoes and gnocchi and bring to a simmer. Bubble for 10 to 15 minutes, stirring occasionally, until the gnocchi are soft and the sauce has thickened. Season, stir in the basil, then transfer to a large ovenproof dish.

Scatter with the mozzarella, then broil for 5 to 6 minutes until the cheese is bubbling and golden.

LOWER CARB RECIPES

Most of your meals will be drawn from this menu; the two meals you eat on rest days and one of your two meals on training days. These recipes are designed to be packed full of nutrients and eating predominately lower carb will increase your chances of burning fat!

Mushrooms are packed full of B vitamins, which help with the breakdown of fat and carbohydrates in the body to provide energy. They also contain betaglucans, which are thought to help boost immunity and aid resistance against allergies. The selenium and ergothioneine (an amino acid) may also help to protect our cells from damage that causes chronic disease.

MUSHROOM OMELET

SERVES: 1
PREP: 5 MINUTES
COOKING: 5 MINUTES

1 tablespoon grass-fed butter
½ cup mushrooms (any variety), sliced
salt and freshly ground black pepper
3 large eggs, free range and preferably organic
1 cup freshly grated Parmesan cheese
a handful of flat-leaf parsley, finely chopped, to garnish

Melt the butter in a frying pan over medium heat. Add the mushrooms and season with salt and pepper.

While the mushrooms are cooking, lightly whisk the eggs. Pour the eggs over the mushrooms, then top with the Parmesan and reduce the heat (eggs cook best with residual heat). Cook for a minute or two, then, using a spatula, ease around the edges of the omelet and fold one half over the other. When the omelet starts to turn golden brown underneath, slide the it onto a plate and garnish with parsley.

Serve with your choice of leafy greens.

The simple things work, but I love to enhance them as much as possible. The first step here is to source the bacon and eggs from your local farmers' market or, even better, directly from a farm stand. Free-range hens that eat a healthy, natural diet pass on that benefit to you in the form of more nutritious and tasty eggs.

CLASSIC BACON AND POACHED EGGS

SERVES: 1
PREP: 2 MINUTES
COOKING: 7 MINUTES

5 cherry tomatoes, halved
salt and freshly ground black pepper
1 tablespoon dried oregano
1 tablespoon extra virgin olive oil
3 thick slices of bacon, preferably organic
2 to 3 large eggs, free range and preferably organic
¼ cup freshly grated Parmesan cheese

Preheat the broiler to high.

Sprinkle the tomatoes with salt, pepper, the oregano, and oil. Place under the broiler with the bacon and cook for 7 minutes, flipping the bacon halfway through cooking.

Meanwhile, heat some water in a saucepan and, when boiling, crack the eggs one at a time into a mug or small glass, then slowly pour them into the water—no swirling or vinegar necessary. Cook for 3 minutes in almost boiling water.

Carefully remove the eggs and place on a plate using a slotted spoon. Season with salt and pepper and sprinkle the Parmesan on top. Serve with the bacon and tomatoes.

I love finding new ways to cook eggs, which are rich in vitamin A. They pair perfectly with smoked salmon—a great source of niacin, which is important for the utilization of energy.

SMOKED SALMON MINI FRITTATAS

SERVES: 2
PREP: 5 MINUTES
COOKING: 20 MINUTES

6 large eggs, free range and preferably organic
¼ cup full-fat Greek yogurt
1 to 2 scallions, finely sliced
2 tablespoons soft goat cheese
1 cup spinach, coarsely chopped
grass-fed butter, for greasing
3½ ounces smoked salmon, cut into thin strips
lemon wedges, to serve

Preheat the oven to 350°F.

Mix the eggs and Greek yogurt together in a bowl. Add the scallions, goat cheese, and spinach.

Grease six small muffin liners with butter and divide the egg mixture equally between them. Bake for 20 minutes until the egg is cooked through.

Place strips of smoked salmon on the top of each egg muffin and serve with lemon wedges on the side.

This dish combines two healthy superpowers: kale and eggs. Kale is a source of vitamins C, K, D, and calcium and iron to name a few. Eggs are one of the most nutritionally dense foods, as they contain a little bit of nearly every nutrient we need for optimal health. Both go perfectly with sun-dried tomatoes, Parmesan, and garlic to make this quick and easy baked dish.

BAKED KALE AND EGGS

SERVES: 1
PREP: 5 MINUTES
COOKING: 15 MINUTES

1 tablespoon grass-fed butter
½ onion, finely chopped
1 garlic clove, finely chopped
2 to 3 handfuls of kale
salt and freshly ground black pepper
2 large eggs, free range and preferably organic
6 sun-dried tomatoes
a handful of freshly grated Parmesan

Preheat the oven to 350°F.

Melt the butter in a large, heatproof frying pan over medium–high heat. Add the onion and garlic and cook, stirring, for about 1 minute. Then add half the kale and sauté, stirring frequently for about 2 minutes until it begins to wilt. Stir in the remaining kale and repeat. Season with salt and pepper, then simmer for about 5 minutes, stirring occasionally, until the kale softens.

Using the back of a spoon, create two pockets in the kale. Crack 1 egg into each pocket. Place the tomatoes around the eggs and sprinkle the Parmesan all over the top to ensure the yolks remain runny. Bake in the oven for 10 minutes and enjoy.

After I traveled to South America I became a little obsessed with guacamole. I tend to serve mine on a bed of spinach and carrots, but you can add it to any salad dish you like. Avocados contain more potassium than bananas, which can help heart function and controls the balance of fluids in the body, which is particularly important after exercising.

EGG GUACAMOLE GOODNESS BOWL

SERVES: 1
PREP: 5 MINUTES
COOKING: 7 MINUTES

2 large eggs, free range and preferably organic
1 whole avocado, peeled and pitted
juice of ½ lime
2 tablespoons cucumber, diced
1 tablespoon full-fat Greek yogurt
salt and freshly ground black pepper
1 medium carrot, grated
1 red bell pepper, thinly sliced
a handful of spinach leaves
cilantro, to garnish

Cook the eggs in boiling water for 7 minutes, then remove from the heat and gradually add cold water to the boiling water so that the eggs don't crack. Let cool in cold water for 5 minutes before peeling.

Mash the avocado in a bowl with the hard-boiled eggs, lime juice, cucumber, and Greek yogurt. Season to taste.

Place the carrot, bell pepper, and spinach in a bowl. Add the avocado mixture, then garnish with cilantro.

This is another great meat-free alternative that's quick to make and full of flavor. Sun-dried tomatoes have a gorgeous, intense taste and are a great source of vitamins C and K, which can help support the immune system and strengthen bones. Try and use those that come in oil, as they're much easier to blend.

GOAT CHEESE AND TOMATO PESTO FRITTATA

SERVES: 2
PREP: 7 MINUTES
COOKING: 5 MINUTES

FOR THE PESTO
a handful of freshly grated Parmesan cheese
a handful of sun-dried tomatoes
a handful of pine nuts
1 garlic clove

FOR THE FRITTATA
1 tablespoon olive oil
1 medium onion, finely chopped
4 large eggs, free range and preferably organic, beaten
¼ cup soft goat cheese
a handful of arugula

Preheat oven to 400°F.

Blend all the pesto ingredients together in a food processor.

For the frittata, heat the oil in an ovenproof frying pan, then cook the onion for about 5 minutes until translucent. Remove the pan from the heat and pour in the beaten eggs.

Place the pan in the oven and cook for 10 to 15 minutes until the eggs are cooked through.

Carefully remove the pan from the oven, cover the frittata with chunks of goat cheese, drizzle with the pesto, and sprinkle the arugula over the top to serve.

These jars are perfect to take to work or enjoy when you're out and about. Shrimp is packed full of protein, contain calcium, potassium, and phosphorus, and are a good source of selenium, magnesium, and zinc, which support the immune system, skin health, and cell reproduction.

SHRIMP SALAD IN A JAR

SERVES: 1
PREP: 10 MINUTES

7 ounces spinach
1 red bell pepper, sliced
1 carrot, peeled and grated
a handful of pine nuts
5 cherry tomatoes, halved
3½ ounces shrimp, cooked and shelled
salt and freshly ground black pepper

FOR THE DRESSING
2 tablespoons extra virgin olive oil
1 tablespoon white wine vinegar
½ tablespoon Dijon mustard

Layer the salad ingredients in the jar in the order given above, adding a bit of salt and pepper to each layer.

Mix the dressing ingredients together and store separately.

Pour the dressing over the salad and it's ready to eat.

Zucchini contains antioxidant vitamin C and has high levels of potassium, which can help regulate blood pressure, as well as replenishing potassium lost through exercise. This simple summer salad can be whipped up in no time.

GRILLED ZUCCHINI SALAD WITH ANCHOVIES AND CAPERS

SERVES: 2
PREP: 5 MINUTES
COOKING: 10 MINUTES

4 zucchini, cut into long slices
3 tablespoons extra virgin olive oil
salt and freshly ground black pepper
a handful of flat-leaf parsley, coarsely chopped, plus extra
    to garnish (optional)
2 anchovies, drained (rinsed, if salted) and finely chopped
2 tablespoons capers
juice of ½ lemon
½ cup feta cheese, crumbled

Coat the sliced zucchini in a little olive oil, salt, and pepper. Cook on a grill pan for 5 minutes, turning them halfway through cooking.

Mix the parsley, remaining oil, anchovies, capers, and lemon juice together in a small bowl and set aside.

Mix all the ingredients together in a bowl and serve with the extra parsley to garnish, if you wish.

I love the strong, tangy flavor of goat cheese; it adds a creamy depth to this pork dish. It also contains a lot less lactose than cheese made from cow's milk, making it easier to digest. (Lactose is the natural sugar found in dairy products, and some people have difficulty digesting it.)

PORK TENDERLOIN WITH CREAMY GOAT CHEESE SAUCE

SERVES: 1
PREP: 5 MINUTES
COOKING: 15 MINUTES

¼ cup full-fat Greek yogurt
½ cup soft goat cheese
6 tablespoons extra virgin olive oil
a handful of flat-leaf parsley leaves, coarsely chopped
2 scallions, thinly sliced
salt and freshly ground black pepper
10½ ounces pork tenderloin
2 large tomatoes, halved
3 ounces baby arugula
3 ounces spinach
a handful of pine nuts
juice of ½ lemon

Mix the yogurt, goat cheese, and 2 tablespoons of cold water in a bowl until smooth. Whisk in 3 tablespoons of the oil, the parsley, and scallions. Season with pepper.

Heat a frying pan over medium–high heat. Brush the pork with 1 tablespoon of the oil and sprinkle with salt and pepper. Cook for 12 to 15 minutes until charred on all sides. Remove from the pan and rest for 10 minutes, then slice thinly.

Meanwhile, brush the cut side of the tomatoes with 1 tablespoon of oil and sprinkle liberally with salt and pepper. Place the tomatoes, cut-side down, into a frying pan and cook for 3 to 4 minutes until charred and the top of the flesh is just softened.

Toss the baby arugula, spinach, and pine nuts with the remaining oil and the lemon juice in a bowl. Season with salt and pepper. Place the pork slices on top of the salad, drizzle with the goat cheese sauce, and serve with the tomatoes on the side.

This simple dish couldn't be any tastier. Try to get organic dairy products from grass-fed cows if you can, as they contain lots more vitamins and minerals than the standard corn-fed varieties. Several studies have found that organic milk has more fat-soluble nutrients—omega-3 fatty acid, vitamin E, and beta-carotene—than non-organic milk, as well as a healthier omega 3:6 ratio.

CHICKEN WITH CREAMY BACON AND MUSHROOM SAUCE

SERVES: 1
PREP: 5 MINUTES
COOKING: 25 MINUTES

FOR THE CHICKEN
4 chicken thighs, skin on
salt and freshly ground black pepper
1 tablespoon Italian herb seasoning
1 tablespoon extra virgin olive oil

FOR THE SAUCE
1 tablespoon extra virgin olive oil
2½ cups button or crimini mushrooms, thinly sliced
5 slices of thick-cut bacon, cooked and diced
¾ cup heavy cream
5 sprigs of thyme leaves, snipped

Preheat the oven to 350°F.

Season the chicken thighs generously with salt and pepper and the Italian herb seasoning mix. Heat the oil over medium–high heat in a large frying pan. Add the chicken thighs, skin-side down, and cook for about 5 minutes until browned. Transfer the chicken, skin-side up, to a foil-lined baking sheet and roast for 20 minutes or until completely cooked through and no longer pink in the center.

Meanwhile, make the sauce: Heat the oil in a large frying pan over medium heat. Add the mushrooms and cook for 3 minutes. Add the bacon, heavy cream, some salt, and thyme. Bring to a boil, stir, then reduce the heat to very low. Simmer for about 2 minutes. (Taste and add more salt if necessary.)

Add the cooked chicken to the pan and spoon the sauce and mushrooms over the top. Serve with your choice of leafy greens.

I absolutely love pizza, but unfortunately it isn't the sort of food you should eat regularly. These eggplant pizzas, however, satisfy the craving with none of the guilt or potential side effects of eating pizza. They are also gluten-free, meat-free, and low-carb, so are a great option for anyone who is avoiding these foods.

EGGPLANT MINI PIZZAS

SERVES: 2
PREP: 30 MINUTES
COOKING: 25 MINUTES

FOR THE SAUCE
2 to 3 tablespoons extra virgin olive oil
3 large garlic cloves, very finely chopped
1 x 14-ounce can chopped tomatoes
1 teaspoon dried Italian seasoning
1 teaspoon dried oregano

FOR THE PIZZAS
2 tablespoons olive oil
1 large eggplant, cut into ¾-inch slices, salted for 30 minutes then dried
1 teaspoon dried Italian seasoning
a handful of basil leaves, chopped
1 cup freshly grated Parmesan cheese
9 ounces good-quality buffalo mozzarella, cut into thick slices

Preheat the oven to 375°F.

Start by making the sauce: Heat the oil in a deep frying pan over medium heat and sauté the garlic until it becomes fragrant; don't let it brown. Add the tomatoes, Italian seasoning, and oregano and simmer until thickened, breaking up the tomatoes as they cook. Add a little water if the sauce gets too thick.

Line a roasting pan with foil. Grease it with a little oil, then lay the eggplant slices on top. Brush the slices with a little more oil and sprinkle with the Italian seasoning. Roast for about 25 minutes.

Remove the eggplant from the oven and layer the sauce, basil, Parmesan, and mozzarella on top. Return to the oven and cook for 2 to 3 minutes until the cheese has melted. Serve immediately.

Serve this rich beef dish with some dark, leafy greens for a quick, filling, and tasty meal that's naturally packed with healthy proteins and contains omega-6 fatty acid to keep you satisfied for longer. Grass-fed beef is lower in saturated fat than standard corn-fed beef, so try to use it if available.

BEEF STROGANOFF

SERVES: 2
PREP: 5 MINUTES
COOKING: 20 MINUTES

9 ounces beef sirloin, cut into ¼ to ½-inch slices and
   then into ½-inch strips
salt and freshly ground black pepper
1 teaspoon paprika
juice of 1 lemon
1 tablespoon grass-fed butter
1 red onion, finely chopped
2 handfuls of shiitake mushrooms, coarsely chopped
1 garlic clove, finely chopped
1 tablespoon English mustard
¾ cup beef stock
¼ cup sour cream
olive oil
a splash of brandy
2 to 3 sprigs of flat-leaf parsley, finely chopped

Season the meat with salt and pepper, the paprika, and lemon juice and set it aside for a few minutes.

Heat the butter in a large frying pan. Add the onion and sauté for 2 minutes, then add the mushrooms and garlic and cook for 5 minutes until both are soft. Stir the mustard into the pan, coating the onion and mushrooms thoroughly. Pour in the stock, then allow to simmer until the liquid has reduced by about half. Stir in the sour cream and set aside for a few minutes.

Heat a little olive oil in a separate pan and cook the beef strips for 1 minute, turning, until browned, but still pink in the middle. Stir in the mushroom and onion mixture, add the brandy, and reduce for 1 minute or until almost evaporated. Garnish with the parsley. Serve with your choice of dark, leafy greens.

These burgers are great to make in advance as they will keep in the fridge for a few days. All you need to do is prepare a quick fresh salad and grab the burgers for a fast and easy lunch on the go. The best thing about them is that, unlike a lot of burgers, these don't contain any bread crumbs and so are just made up of lean protein.

TERIYAKI TURKEY BURGERS

SERVES: 2
PREP: 10 MINUTES
COOKING: 10 MINUTES

9 ounces ground turkey
1 teaspoon grated fresh ginger
2 tablespoons teriyaki glaze (available from most supermarkets)
salt and freshly ground black pepper
2 pineapple rings
2 slices of Cheddar cheese
¾ cup sliced cucumber
2 handfuls of arugula
1 red bell pepper, finely sliced
1 avocado, peeled, pitted, and chopped into ¾-inch cubes

FOR THE DRESSING
3 tablespoons teriyaki sauce
2 tablespoons rice vinegar or apple cider vinegar
3 tablespoons olive oil
1 tablespoon pineapple juice (from the can of pineapple rings)

Preheat the broiler to medium–high. Mix together the turkey, ginger, and teriyaki glaze and season well. Shape into 2 burgers.

Broil the burgers for about 5 minutes on each side, brushing with any remaining teriyaki glaze, until done as desired. Broil the pineapple slices at the same time and cook until lightly golden brown. Turn off the broiler, place the cheese slices on top of the burgers, and let them melt in the residual heat.

Meanwhile, mix all the dressing ingredients with the cucumber, arugula, red bell pepper, and avocado.

Serve the burgers topped with the grilled pineapple rings and the salad alongside.

Beet and goat cheese are a perfect pair. Health studies suggest that beets can help lower blood pressure, boost performance in exercise, and help prevent dementia. Plus, they are a great source of betaine, which is thought to help fight inflammation, protect internal organs, and improve vascular risk factors like heart disease.

BAKED BEET, WALNUT, AND GOAT CHEESE SALAD

SERVES: 2
PREP: 5 MINUTES
COOKING: 20 MINUTES

9 ounces raw beets, peeled and cut into wedges
4 tablespoons extra virgin olive oil
3 tablespoons balsamic vinegar
salt and freshly ground black pepper
7 ounces green beans, trimmed
5½ ounces arugula
3½-ounce round of goat cheese, cut into 6 rounds
½ cup walnuts, coarsely chopped

Preheat the oven to 400°F.

Put the beets in a roasting pan with 1 tablespoon of the oil, 1 tablespoon of the vinegar, and plenty of salt and pepper. Roast for 8 to 10 minutes until sticky.

Meanwhile, bring a pan of salted water to a boil, add the green beans, cook for 1 minute, then drain. Toss in with the beets and roast for another 5 minutes.

Make the dressing by combining the remaining oil and vinegar in a small bowl and season well. Put the arugula in a bowl and toss with a little dressing.

Dip the cheese rounds in the chopped walnuts, so the tops are covered, then pop in the roasting pan with the beets and green beans and cook for another few minutes to soften and toast the nuts.

Pile the salad onto plates and serve with the remaining dressing drizzled over the top.

This dish is so cheap and packed full of flavor and crunchy vegetables with a distinctive Thai taste from the coconut cream. Plus, the zucchini, red bell pepper, broccoli, and green beans are loaded with vitamins A, C, and K, which help keep your immune system, bones, and white blood cells healthy.

THAI GREEN CHICKEN CURRY

SERVES: 2
PREP: 5 MINUTES
COOKING: 10 MINUTES

2 tablespoons olive oil
1 red chile, sliced
1 tablespoon Thai green curry paste
1 skinless chicken breast, cut into 1¼-inch cubes
1¼ cups coconut cream
1¼ cups snow peas
1 red bell pepper, sliced
¾ cup green beans
¾ cup broccoli, broken into small florets
1 zucchini, diced
a handful of chopped cilantro, to serve (optional)

Heat a wok over high heat and add the oil, chile, and Thai green curry paste. Cook for 2 minutes, then add the chicken and cook for another 5 minutes until brown all over.

Add the coconut cream and all the vegetables and cook for 5 to 10 minutes over high heat, or until vegetables are cooked. Garnish with cilantro, if you wish, and serve.

I've been trying to embrace eating more meat-free meals. This is healthier, better for the environment, and means being a little bit more creative in the culinary department. Portobello mushrooms are a great option since they have a wonderfully meaty texture after they've been roasted. They also contain selenium which is thought to improve immune response.

BLUE-CHEESE-STUFFED PORTOBELLO MUSHROOMS

SERVES: 1
PREP: 5 MINUTES
COOKING: 16 MINUTES

2 portobello mushrooms, stems removed and chopped
3 tablespoons unsalted, grass-fed butter
salt and freshly ground black pepper
2 sprigs of thyme
1 tablespoon olive oil
½ onion, finely sliced
2 garlic cloves, finely chopped
¼ cup blue cheese
¼ cup chives, chopped

Preheat the oven to 400°F.

Put the mushrooms on a baking sheet, flat-side up. Divide the unsalted butter between the mushrooms, season with salt and pepper, and put a sprig of thyme on each one. Bake for 10 minutes.

Heat the oil in a frying pan, add the onion and garlic, and cook until soft. Add the chopped mushroom stems and a grinding of black pepper and cook until softened.

Spoon the mixture into the baked mushrooms and scatter the blue cheese on top. Roast for another 6 minutes or until the tops are golden and bubbling.

Put the mushrooms on a serving plate, sprinkle with the chives, and serve with your choice of leafy greens.

This dish couldn't be any simpler to make and is full of authentic Asian flavors that complement the tuna perfectly. Try to source the freshest fish possible; two ways of telling whether it is fresh are the smell—a fresh fish should not smell "fishy"—and the look of the eyes, which should be clear, not cloudy. Fresh fish tastes so much better and has more nutritional content than frozen.

SEARED TUNA AND CRUNCHY ASIAN ASPARAGUS SALAD

SERVES: 1
PREP: 5 MINUTES
COOKING: 5 MINUTES

7 ounces yellowfin tuna steak (sustainably sourced)
2 tablespoons black and white sesame seeds
salt and freshly ground black pepper
2 tablespoons toasted sesame oil
3½ ounces broccolini, cut into 1¼-inch slices
1 bok choy, cut into 1¼-inch slices
3½ ounces asparagus, cut into 1¼-inch slices
2 tablespoons dark or light soy sauce
2 tablespoons teriyaki sauce
3 tablespoons pickled ginger
1 red chile, finely chopped
juice of ½ lemon

Roll and press the tuna into the sesame seeds seasoned with a little salt and pepper. Set aside.

Heat a frying pan and a wok over high heat and add 1 tablespoon of oil to each.

Sear the tuna in the frying pan for 20 seconds on each side. Put the vegetables and soy and teriyaki sauces in the wok and cook for 5 minutes. Remove the tuna from the pan and cut into even ¾-inch slices.

Place the tuna on a large plate and cover with the ginger and chile, then drizzle with the lemon juice.

Serve the vegetables alongside the tuna.

Cauliflower rice has become increasingly popular over the past few years as people have started noticing what a great alternative it is to actual rice. I now prefer the cauliflower kind over the white starchy variety I was once used to. I find it's best to cook it in butter for a few minutes to get the best taste and texture.

SHRIMP AND TOMATO CURRY

SERVES: 2
PREP: 5 MINUTES
COOKING: 20 MINUTES

FOR THE CAULIFLOWER RICE
2 garlic cloves, crushed
½ cauliflower, broken into small florets
½ onion
1 tablespoon fresh ginger
1 teaspoon sesame oil
2 tablespoons grass-fed butter
2 tablespoons sugar-free fish sauce

FOR THE CURRY
2 tablespoons olive oil
½ large onion, thinly sliced
2 garlic cloves, sliced
1 green chile, seeded and sliced
3 tablespoons curry paste
1 tablespoon tomato paste
½ cup vegetable stock
½ cup coconut cream
7 ounces raw shrimp
cilantro, finely chopped, to garnish

To make the cauliflower rice, put the garlic, cauliflower, onion, and ginger into a food processor and blend. Set aside.

Now move on to the sauce: Heat the oil in a large frying pan. Cook the onion, garlic, and half the chile for 5 minutes. Add the curry paste and cook for another minute. Then add the tomato paste, stock, and coconut cream. Simmer for 10 minutes.

Back to the cauliflower rice: heat the oil and butter in a separate frying pan and cook the cauliflower mixture for 3 minutes, then add the fish sauce and reduce. Set aside, keeping it warm.

Add the shrimp to the curry. Cook for 3 minutes or until the shrimp turns opaque. Scatter with the remaining chile and cilantro, and serve with the cauliflower rice.

This recipe requires no cooking, so there's no room for excuses here! Tuna is an excellent source of potassium and B vitamins, meaning it is great for heart health. I always have cans of tuna in the cupboard—it's a great lean protein that you can make incredibly quick meals and snacks with when you're in a hurry.

TUNA LETTUCE CUPS

SERVES: 1
PREP: 10 MINUTES

5½-ounce can tuna, drained
1 tablespoon full-fat Greek yogurt
½ red onion, finely chopped
2 scallions, finely chopped
3 gherkins, finely chopped
1 tablespoon cream cheese (optional)
juice of ½ lemon
salt and freshly ground black pepper
1 head romaine lettuce

Mix the tuna in a bowl with the Greek yogurt, onion, scallions, gherkins, cream cheese (if using), and lemon juice. Season with salt and pepper.

Pull out the large leaves of the lettuce and scoop 2 to 3 tablespoons of the tuna mixture onto each leaf.

The Mediterranean diet is hailed as one of the healthiest on earth. Use good-quality chicken and make this gorgeous Mediterranean-inspired sauce using some of the favorite ingredients of the region—lemon and yogurt. Full-fat yogurt is loaded with calcium, protein, and probiotics. Make sure you always go for full-fat as the low-fat options often have lots of added sugars.

CHICKEN BREAST WITH A LEMON YOGURT SAUCE

SERVES: 1
PREP: 2 MINUTES
COOKING: 20 MINUTES

1 large chicken breast, skin on
2 teaspoons paprika
2 tablespoons olive oil
salt and freshly ground black pepper
2 tablespoons full-fat Greek yogurt
2 scallions, finely chopped
juice of ½ lemon
1 tablespoon grass-fed butter
7 ounces spring greens, finely chopped

Marinate the chicken in the paprika and 1 tablespoon of oil. Season with salt and pepper and set aside.

Heat the remaining oil in a frying pan over medium–high heat. Add the breast and cook for 15 to 20 minutes, turning every few minutes until the chicken is cooked through and slightly browned on the outside.

Meanwhile, mix the yogurt with the scallions, lemon juice, and a little salt and black pepper. Set aside.

In a separate pan, heat the butter over medium–high heat. Add the spring greens, season with salt and black pepper, and cook for 5 to 8 minutes until the leaves have wilted.

Serve the chicken on top of the greens and drizzle the yogurt sauce over the top.

I love Italian food. They keep things simple when it comes to cooking, letting the flavors from quality ingredients speak for themselves. Lamb is full of vitamin B12 and iron, which help to keep your nervous system and red blood cells healthy.

ITALIAN LAMB CHOPS

SERVES: 2
PREP: 5 MINUTES
COOKING: 15 MINUTES

2 tablespoons extra virgin olive oil
2 x 1½-inch thick lamb loin chops, weighing about 9 ounces each
1 teaspoon paprika
salt and freshly ground black pepper
4 shallots, halved
1 tablespoon grass-fed butter or coconut oil
14 ounces kale
4 plum tomatoes, quartered
a handful of Kalamata olives, pitted
a handful of flat-leaf parsley, chopped

Preheat the oven to 400°F.

Heat 1 tablespoon of the olive oil in a large, ovenproof frying pan over medium–high heat. Season the lamb with the remaining oil, the paprika, salt, and pepper and cook for 2 to 3 minutes per side until browned.

Add the shallots to the pan, transfer to the oven, and cook the lamb as desired (6 to 8 minutes for medium-rare).

While the lamb is cooking, heat the butter or coconut oil in a frying pan and cook the kale for 5 to 7 minutes with plenty of salt, so it gets crispy.

Add the tomatoes, olives, and parsley to the lamb and toss with the shallots to combine.

Serve the lamb with the Mediterranean veggies scattered on top and the kale on the side.

Salmon is an excellent source of vitamin B12, which is needed for the growth and formation of red blood cells and a healthy nervous system. It also tastes great, and this is an incredibly simple way to cook it, so your meal is on the table in little over 20 minutes.

CHILE-COVERED SALMON WITH SPINACH

SERVES: 2
PREP: 5 MINUTES
COOKING: 20 MINUTES

2 salmon fillets
2 red chiles, finely chopped
½ onion, finely chopped
1 garlic clove, finely chopped
1 tablespoon olive oil
salt and freshly ground black pepper
4 very thin slices of lemon
1 tablespoon grass-fed butter
14 ounces spinach

Preheat the oven to 400°F.

Place the salmon fillets on individual 8-inch squares of foil.

In a small bowl, mix the chiles, onion, garlic, and oil together.

Season the fillets with salt and pepper, then top with the chile mixture and place the lemon slices on top. Wrap the fillets in the foil and roast for 20 minutes.

After 15 minutes, melt the butter in a frying pan over medium heat then add the spinach. Season with salt and pepper and cook for 5 minutes until wilted.

Remove the salmon from the oven, unwrap it, and remove the lemon slices. Serve with the spinach.

Who doesn't love one-pan dishes? It's great being able to throw a few ingredients into a pan, do almost no work, and get a dish packed with flavor at the end. I love using beans in dishes with a tomato-sauce base—they seem to just suck up all the flavor of the sauce—and they are also loaded with vitamin E and contain some selenium.

ONE-PAN CHORIZO WITH BEANS

SERVES: 2
PREP: 2 MINUTES
COOKING: 20 MINUTES

5½ ounces smoked, fresh chorizo sausage, casing removed
1 onion, chopped
2 ribs of celery, chopped
1 red bell pepper, sliced
1 garlic clove, chopped
¾ cup dry white wine
1 x 7-ounce can plum tomatoes
1 cup canned cannellini beans or chickpeas, drained and rinsed
a handful chopped flat-leaf parsley, to garnish
salt and freshly ground black pepper

Cook the chorizo in a large frying pan until it releases its oil. Add the onion, celery, red bell pepper, and garlic and cook until softened.

Stir in the wine and tomatoes. Season and simmer for 15 minutes until the sauce thickens, stirring occasionally to break up the tomatoes.

Add the beans and simmer for another 5 minutes. Sprinkle with the parsley and serve hot, or just warm, in a bowl.

This is a great alternative to some of your favorite pasta dishes. Eggplant is one of the most versatile vegetables. This dish is deliciously cheesy and oozes when it comes out of the oven. Make sure you always keep the skin on an eggplant as this contains essential micronutrients like vitamin E, which helps to strengthen the immune system.

EGGPLANT PARMIGIANA WITH MEDITERRANEAN SALAD

SERVES: 4
PREP: 5 MINUTES
COOKING: 1 HOUR

3 eggplant, cut into ½-inch thick slices
5 to 8 tablespoons extra virgin olive oil
1 onion, diced
2 garlic cloves, finely chopped
½ cup basil, roughly torn, plus a few leaves to garnish
3 cups good-quality tomato sauce (no added sugar)
9 ounces good-quality mozzarella, drained and torn
a handful of freshly grated Parmesan cheese

FOR THE SALAD
2 handfuls of arugula
a handful of black olives, pitted
8 cherry tomatoes, quartered
½ large cucumber, diced
½ red onion, thinly sliced
1 tablespoon olive oil
2 tablespoons white wine vinegar
salt and freshly ground black pepper

Preheat the broiler to high. Toss the eggplant with some of the oil and place on a baking sheet. Broil, in batches if necessary, for 4 to 5 minutes on each side until nicely browned. Set aside.

Meanwhile, heat 1 tablespoon of oil in a saucepan and cook the onion, garlic, and half the torn basil for 3 to 4 minutes until golden. Add the sauce and simmer for 5 minutes.

Preheat the oven to 350°F. In a heatproof dish, layer the eggplant, tomato sauce, mozzarella, then the remaining torn basil. Repeat until all the ingredients have been used. Sprinkle the Parmesan on top and bake for 40 to 45 minutes until golden and bubbling. Scatter with a few leaves of basil to garnish.

For the salad, mix the arugula, olives, tomatoes, cucumber, and onion together in a large bowl. Drizzle with the oil and vinegar and season well with salt and pepper.

This is perhaps one of the quickest and easiest dishes you will ever make, yet one of the tastiest. The pancetta gives a rich, salty flavor that perfectly complements the scallops. Spinach boasts an endless list of vitamins and minerals—including potassium, manganese, zinc, magnesium, iron, calcium, and folate.

SCALLOPS WITH PANCETTA AND SPINACH

SERVES: 1
PREP: 2 MINUTES
COOKING: 4 MINUTES

1 tablespoon extra virgin olive oil
½ teaspoon Dijon mustard
1 teaspoon white wine vinegar
freshly ground black pepper
¾ cup spinach leaves
3 tablespoons crème fraîche
juice of ¼ lemon
¼ cup pancetta, diced
6 large fresh scallops

In a large bowl, whisk together the oil, mustard, and vinegar and season with black pepper. Drizzle this over the spinach on a plate.

In a separate bowl, mix the crème fraîche with half the lemon juice. Set aside.

Heat a frying pan until hot. Add the pancetta and cook for 2 minutes until it begins to release some fat, then add the scallops and cook for another 30 seconds to 1 minute on each side, until opaque and just cooked through. Add the remaining lemon juice to the pan.

Place the scallops on top of the spinach leaves and spoon over the pancetta and pan juices. Drizzle the lemon and crème fraîche mixture over the top.

I've mentioned previously my love for pesto; it's just such a versatile sauce that goes with almost any dish. It's particularly good when paired with fish. Oily fish with its high omega-3 content is thought to help cardiovascular health. I try to incorporate it into my diet as much as possible (at least two portions a week) and this recipe is a simple and delicious way of doing so.

BAKED MACKEREL AND GARLIC PESTO

SERVES: 1
PREP: 5 MINUTES
COOKING: 25 MINUTES

2 mackerel fillets
3 slices of lemon
½ red bell pepper, finely chopped
½ red onion, finely chopped
1 zucchini, chopped
1 tablespoon lemon juice
a handful of flat-leaf parsley, chopped
salt and freshly ground black pepper
a handful of arugula

FOR THE PESTO
a handful of basil leaves
1 tablespoon lemon juice
2 tablespoons extra virgin olive oil
1 garlic clove, crushed

Preheat the oven to 350°F.

Put the mackerel fillets skin-side down on a baking sheet and cover the fish with a line of lemon slices. Scatter with the bell pepper, onion, and zucchini, then drizzle with the lemon juice.

Sprinkle with the parsley and season to taste with salt and pepper. Bake for 25 minutes.

While the fish is cooking, make the pesto: Put the basil, lemon juice, oil, and garlic in a small blender or food processor and pulse to a smooth paste.

Remove the fish from the oven, place on top of the arugula leaves with the vegetables, then drizzle with the garlic pesto to serve.

This has become one of my regular go-to dishes when breaking my fast, as it still feels kind of like brunch and, frankly, I can't get enough of eggs. Add as much or as little chile as you like—it contains carotenoids which help to improve insulin regulation.

SHAKSHUKA

SERVES: 2 TO 3
PREP: 5 MINUTES
COOKING: 25 MINUTES

2 tablespoons olive oil
½ onion, diced
1 garlic clove, finely chopped
1 red bell pepper, diced
2 x 14-ounce cans chopped tomatoes
1 teaspoon chili powder
1 teaspoon ground cumin
1 teaspoon paprika
salt and freshly ground black pepper
5 large eggs, free range and preferably organic
a handful of flat-leaf parsley, finely chopped, to garnish

Slowly warm the oil in a large, deep saucepan over medium heat. Add the onion and cook for a few minutes until it begins to soften, then add the garlic and sauté for another 2 minutes. Add the bell pepper and cook for 5 to 7 minutes until softened. Add the tomatoes and stir until combined. Stir in the spices and simmer for 5 to 7 minutes until the sauce starts to reduce.

At this point, you can taste the mixture and adjust the spices according to your preference. Add salt and pepper to taste or more chile (if you like spice!).

Crack the eggs, one at a time, directly over the tomato mixture, making sure to space them evenly apart. I usually place 4 eggs around the outer edge and one in the center.

Cover the pan. Simmer for 10 to 15 minutes or until the eggs are cooked and the sauce has slightly reduced. Keep an eye on the pan to make sure that the sauce doesn't reduce too much, which can lead to burning. Serve immediately, garnished with parsley.

This dish can be enjoyed alone or with poached eggs, if you feel the need. Swiss chard is a great base for any dish as it tends to be more mild in flavor when compared with its leafy-green cousins. When buying Swiss chard, look for vibrant color and unbruised leaves and stems. The leaves should not be wilted. Swiss chard contains very high amounts of vitamin K, which is essential for healthy blood clotting and bones.

CREAMED SWISS CHARD WITH PINE NUTS

SERVES: 1
PREP: 2 MINUTES
COOKING: 10 MINUTES

2 tablespoons pine nuts
1 tablespoon grass-fed butter
½ red onion, diced
1 large bunch of rainbow or Swiss chard, coarsely chopped
salt and freshly ground black pepper
6 tablespoons cream cheese
1 teaspoon freshly grated nutmeg
2 poached eggs (optional)

Heat a pan over medium–high heat. Dry-fry the pine nuts for 3 to 5 minutes, constantly shaking them in the pan. Once they begin to brown, add the butter, wait for it to melt, then add the onion. Cook until the onion starts to become translucent, then add the chard and season with salt and pepper. Cook for 5 to 7 minutes until the chard starts to wilt.

Meanwhile, combine the cream cheese, nutmeg, and 2 tablespoons of water in a medium saucepan. Place over medium heat and cook, whisking frequently, until the cheese melts and the mixture just bubbles around the edges. Using a slotted spoon, transfer the chard to the pan with the cheese mixture, leaving any excess liquid in the pan. Mix well and season with salt and pepper.

Top this off with two poached eggs, if you want to make a meal that is a bit more filling.

To poach the eggs, boil some water in a pan then reduce the heat to a simmer. Crack one egg into a cup and carefully pour the egg into the water. Repeat with the other egg and cook both for 3 minutes. Carefully scoop the eggs out using a slotted spoon.

One serving of trout is thought to contain seven of the B-complex vitamins that help to convert the food you eat into energy. Serve this trout in a deliciously creamy sauce and be sure to add a squeeze of lemon over the top.

TROUT WITH BACON AND PEAS

SERVES: 1
PREP: 7 MINUTES
COOKING: 15 MINUTES

FOR THE DRESSING
a handful of flat-leaf parsley
a handful of mint
a handful of basil
pinch of salt
1 teaspoon English mustard
1 tablespoon organic cider
 vinegar
½ cup canola oil

FOR THE SAUCE
¼ cup white wine
1 garlic clove, finely sliced
sprig of thyme
¼ cup fish stock
¼ cup heavy cream
2 tablespoons grass-fed butter

FOR THE TROUT
2 tablespoons canola oil, plus
 extra for the fish
2 to 3 slices thick-cut bacon,
 cut into ¼-inch strips
¼ cup fresh peas
salt and freshly ground black
 pepper
1 scallion, finely chopped
7 ounces wild sea trout fillet
2 baby gem lettuce, separated
 into leaves

Start by making the dressing: Place the herbs in a mortar with the salt and mustard. Pound to a paste, then add the vinegar and oil.

To make the sauce, put the wine, garlic, and thyme in a saucepan over high heat and reduce for 5 minutes. Add the fish stock, reduce by half, then add the cream and bring to a boil. Finally, whisk in the butter.

Heat the oil in a separate pan and fry the bacon until golden. Add the peas, season with salt and pepper, and then pour in the reduced fish sauce. Boil for 5 minutes, then add the scallion.

Pour a little oil onto a grill pan, season the trout, and cook for 2 minutes, skin-side down. Flip over and cook for 2 minutes.

To serve, place a few lettuce leaves on a plate, spoon on the peas, bacon, and fish sauce, place the fish on top, and drizzle with the herb dressing.

I recently visited Rome where I fell in love with this pesto. The sun-dried tomatoes make any simple recipe extra tasty and give this a real hit of flavor. I particularly like eating the pesto with spiralized zucchini, a source of vitamins K and C, which help with immune function. It also has the look and texture of pasta or noodles but without the potential blood-sugar spikes.

CHICKEN AND SUN-DRIED TOMATO PESTO ZUCCHINI NOODLES

SERVES: 1
PREP: 8 MINUTES
COOKING: 10 MINUTES

olive oil
1 chicken breast, skin on, cut into 1¼-inch cubes
3 zucchini, spiralized or cut into ribbons using a peeler

FOR THE PESTO
a handful of sun-dried tomatoes
a handful of basil, plus extra to garnish
a handful of freshly grated Parmesan cheese
a handful of pine nuts
2 tablespoons extra virgin olive oil
salt and freshly ground black pepper

Heat a drizzle of oil in a pan over medium heat. Add the chicken and cook for 5 to 7 minutes, stirring every minute or so, until it is cooked through.

Meanwhile, put all the pesto ingredients in a food processor and pulse-blend until smooth. You can add more olive oil if the mixture looks too thick.

Put the spiralized zucchini in a dry wok or pan over high heat. Cook for 2 minutes.

Once the "noodles" are cooked, remove from the heat and mix in the pesto and chicken. Serve with extra basil scattered over the top.

This vinaigrette is incredibly versatile and can be used as a sauce, dressing, or marinade. In this dish it's paired with beautifully wilted Swiss chard, which contains around 13 different compounds with antioxidant properties. This dish is extremely quick to make and can be on the table in 15 minutes.

ROUND STEAK WITH AN HERB VINAIGRETTE AND CHARD

SERVES: 1
PREP: 5 MINUTES
COOKING: 10 MINUTES

FOR THE VINAIGRETTE
1 shallot, finely chopped
3 small gherkins, finely chopped
a handful of cilantro, finely chopped
a handful of chives, finely chopped
1 teaspoon Dijon mustard
2 teaspoons white wine vinegar
1 teaspoon honey
¼ cup canola oil
1 teaspoon capers

FOR THE STEAK
2 tablespoons grass-fed butter
1 tablespoon extra virgin olive oil
9-ounce grass-fed round steak
7 ounces Swiss chard
salt and freshly ground black pepper

In a bowl combine all the vinaigrette ingredients and set aside.

Heat a frying pan until hot, then add the half the butter and the oil. Add the steak and cook on one side for 2 minutes (without moving the steak), or until browned. Turn the steak over and cook for another 2 minutes, then remove the pan from the heat and set the steak aside to rest.

Heat the remaining butter in a saucepan and cook the chard for 5 minutes until wilted. Season with salt and pepper.

Serve the steak on a plate, drizzled with the vinaigrette and with the chard on the side.

Sauce vierge is a French sauce made from olive oil, lemon juice, chopped tomatoes, and chopped basil. Tomatoes contain lycopene, which has antioxidant properties that help to combat the formation of free radicals, which cause oxidative stress.

SEA BASS WITH SAUCE VIERGE

SERVES: 1
PREP: 5 MINUTES
COOKING: 10 MINUTES

a handful of cherry tomatoes, halved
1 shallot, diced
2 tablespoons capers
juice of ½ lemon
2 tablespoons extra virgin olive oil
salt and freshly ground black pepper
1 tablespoon olive oil
2 sea bass fillets, skin on
7 ounces spinach

Put the tomatoes and shallot in a pan with the capers, lemon juice, and extra virgin olive oil. Season with salt and pepper.

Meanwhile, add the olive oil to a separate pan over high heat and cook the sea bass for 5 to 7 minutes, skin-side down, until just cooked and the flesh is white.

Meanwhile, warm the sauce through for 2 minutes. Cook the spinach with salt and pepper for 2 minutes until wilted.

Transfer the sea bass onto the spinach and drizzle the sauce over the top of the fish.

This mayo-free Asian slaw adds a twist to the version you're probably used to. White cabbage is a bit of an unsung hero. It's full of vitamin K, which helps keep bones strong and it's also a great source of vitamin C, essential for protecting cells and keeping them healthy.

PORK CHOP WITH PEANUT BUTTER SATAY AND AN ASIAN SLAW

SERVES: 1
PREP: 10 MINUTES
COOKING: 10 MINUTES

2 tablespoons grass-fed butter
3 teaspoons soy sauce
1 garlic clove, finely chopped
9 ounce pork chop
1 tablespoon peanut butter (no added sugar or oil)
1 tablespoon honey
1 tablespoon boiling water
2 carrots, peeled and grated
¾ cup white cabbage, grated
a handful of mint, finely chopped
a handful of cilantro, finely chopped

FOR THE DRESSING
1 garlic clove, finely chopped
1 to 2 red chiles, sliced
1 tablespoon red wine vinegar
1 tablespoon fish sauce
1 tablespoon lime juice
2 tablespoons toasted sesame oil

Melt the butter in a frying pan and mix in half the soy sauce. Sauté the garlic until lightly browned.

Place the pork chop in the pan, cover, and cook for 8 to 10 minutes on each side.

Meanwhile, combine the peanut butter, remaining soy sauce, honey, and boiling water together in a small bowl.

Put the carrots and cabbage into a large bowl, and add the mint and cilantro.

To make the dressing, mix the garlic, chiles, vinegar, fish sauce, lime juice, and sesame oil together. Drizzle the dressing over the slaw and serve with the pork and satay sauce.

HEALTHIER SNACKS

Healthier snacks are completely optional. You can have one snack between your two meals if you wish. For example, if you skip breakfast you can have one snack between lunch and dinner and if you skip dinner, then have a snack between breakfast and lunch. If you do snack between meals, your snacks need to be as filling and nutritious as possible. A lot of these recipes can be made in bulk over the weekend so you have them ready in the fridge to eat during the week. This will mean you are much less likely to snack on any cheap, processed convenience food.

I love guacamole and I love tuna. I tried combining the two and it tastes great! It works perfectly as a snack because it's so filling. Avocado is packed full of healthy fats and tuna is full of protein, meaning there will be no blood-sugar spikes after eating it.

TUNA GUACAMOLE

SERVES: 2
PREP: 10 MINUTES

1 x 5½-ounce can of tuna, drained
1 avocado, peeled, pitted, and coarsely chopped
1 tablespoon full-fat Greek yogurt
1 tablespoon lemon juice
salt and freshly ground black pepper

Mix all the ingredients together in a bowl. Eat by itself or use as a dip with your choice of vegetables. Bell peppers and cucumbers work particularly well.

Give yourself no excuse to reach for processed crap! Sun-dried tomatoes contain a decent amount of iron, which plays a role in the production of hemoglobin and red blood cells.

FETA AND SUN-DRIED TOMATO DIP

SERVES: 8
PREP: 5 MINUTES
COOKING: 5 MINUTES

¾ cup feta cheese, crumbled
1 cup full-fat Greek yogurt
2 tablespoons olive oil
¼ cup sun-dried tomatoes, drained
salt and freshly ground black pepper

Place all the ingredients in a food processor and blend together.

Serve with your choice of vegetable sticks. Carrots, cucumber, or bell peppers work well.

Roasted eggplant have an amazingly sweet flavor. They are also a good source of vitamins B1 and B6, which can help to support the immune system. They also contain high levels of manganese, which is essential for the health of our bones.

EGGPLANT DIP

SERVES: 4
PREP: 5 MINUTES
COOKING: 45 MINUTES

1 medium eggplant
1 garlic clove
1 green chile, seeded and finely chopped
1 tablespoon extra virgin olive oil
juice of ½ lemon
½ bunch of flat-leaf parsley, coarsely chopped
salt and freshly ground black pepper
½ teaspoon paprika

Preheat the oven to 350°F.

Pierce the eggplant a couple of times with a knife, place in a roasting pan, then roast for 45 minutes until softened. Let cool.

Once cooled, scoop the insides from the eggplant into a food processor. Blend with the garlic, chile, oil, lemon juice, parsley, and a pinch of salt and black pepper.

Taste and adjust the seasoning, oil, and lemon as needed. Place in a dish and sprinkle with the paprika. Serve with flatbreads.

Once I realized how simple this pâté was to make I became fully addicted to it! It will sit in the fridge for up to five days, so there is no excuse for snacking on anything processed. Oily fish like mackerel are full of omega-3 fatty acids, important for cardiovascular health.

SMOKED MACKEREL PÂTÉ

SERVES: 3
PREP: 10 MINUTES

3 hot-smoked mackerel fillets
¾ cup cream cheese
½ cup crème fraîche
3 teaspoons grated horseradish
freshly ground black pepper
1 lemon, to squeeze
a small handful of dill, finely chopped
2 slices of rye bread

Skin the mackerel fillets. Flake three-quarters into a food processor with the cream cheese, crème fraîche, and horseradish and combine until smooth.

Add a good grinding of black pepper and lemon juice to taste, then fold through the dill and the remaining fish. Serve on rye bread.

After spending some time in Russia I learned to appreciate a good-quality rye bread. It doesn't contain gluten and it doesn't affect your blood-sugar levels nearly as much as white bread made from wheat.

PEANUT BUTTER AND BANANA ON RYE

SERVES: 1
PREP: 5 MINUTES

2 tablespoons peanut butter
2 slices of rye bread
1 banana, peeled and sliced

Spread the peanut butter on the rye bread and top with the slices of banana.

Whoever thought of dipping apples into almond butter was a genius! The almond butter helps to keep you full and the polyphenols, which are plant compounds found in apples, also slow down the digestion of carbs and lower blood-sugar levels.

APPLE WITH ALMOND BUTTER

SERVES: 1
PREP: 5 MINUTES

1 apple
2 to 3 tablespoons almond butter (100 percent almonds)

Slice the apple and dip the slices into the tasty almond butter.

Eggs are a great source of inexpensive quality protein. Source free range and organic, so the eggs are as nutritious as possible.

DEVILED EGGS

SERVES: 3
PREP: 5 MINUTES
COOKING: 8 MINUTES

6 large eggs
¼ cup mayonnaise
1 teaspoon white wine vinegar
1 teaspoon English mustard
salt and freshly ground black pepper
smoked paprika, to garnish

Place the eggs into boiling water and boil for 8 minutes. Gradually fill the pan with cold water, so they don't crack, and then leave in cold water for 5 minutes.

Carefully peel the eggs under cold running water. Gently dry with paper towels. Slice the eggs in half lengthwise. Transfer the yolks to a medium bowl and place the whites on a serving platter. Mash the yolks into a fine crumble using a fork. Add the mayonnaise, vinegar, mustard, salt, and pepper and mix well.

Evenly disperse heaping teaspoons of the yolk mixture into the egg white halves. Sprinkle with paprika and serve.

Greek yogurt is full of protein and fat to keep you fuller for longer, plus the probiotic cultures help to promote good bacteria in the gut, essential for proper absorption of nutrients.

GREEK YOGURT WITH HONEY AND GINGER

SERVES: 1
PREP: 2 MINUTES

1 cup full-fat Greek yogurt
¾-inch piece of fresh ginger, peeled and grated
1 teaspoon honey

Pour the Greek yogurt into a bowl, sprinkle the ginger all over, and drizzle with the honey.

Prepare this at the beginning of the week and you can enjoy it for up to seven days. It is packed full of flavor and nutrients like potassium which can help to regulate blood pressure.

HOMEMADE BEET HUMMUS WITH CARROT STICKS

SERVES: 4
PREP: 10 MINUTES
COOKING: 1 HOUR

1 large beet
4 tablespoons extra virgin olive oil
2½ cups cooked chickpeas, drained
zest of 1 large lemon, plus juice of ½
2 large garlic cloves, minced
2 tablespoons tahini
salt and freshly ground black pepper
carrot sticks, to serve

Preheat the oven to 350°F.

Remove the stem and most of the root from the beet. Scrub and wash it under cold running water until clean.

Place the beet on a piece of foil, drizzle with 1 tablespoon of oil, and wrap tightly. Roast for 1 hour or until a knife can be inserted into the center without resistance. It should be tender. Remove the foil, place in a bowl, and leave in the fridge to cool.

Peel and quarter the beet and place in a food processor. Blend until only small pieces remain. Add the remaining ingredients, except for the oil, and process until smooth. Drizzle in the oil as the hummus is mixing.

Taste and adjust the seasoning as needed, adding more salt, lemon juice, or olive oil if necessary. If the consistency is too thick, add a little water.

The hummus will keep in the fridge for up to a week. Serve with carrot sticks or other vegetables, such as celery, bell pepper, or cucumber.

These chicken skewers are perfect to take into work, giving you a great alternative to the vending machine.

SMOKY CHICKEN SKEWERS

SERVES: 4
PREP: 5 MINUTES
COOKING: 20 MINUTES

3 tablespoons hot sauce
1 tablespoon sesame oil
1 tablespoon paprika
1 tablespoon ground cumin
1¼ pounds skinless chicken breast, chopped into 1¼-inch cubes
2 tablespoons sesame seeds, to garnish
lemon wedges, to serve

Preheat the oven to 400°F.

Make a marinade with the hot sauce, oil, and spices, then cover the chicken with it. Thread on to skewers.

Roast for 16 to 20 minutes. Sprinkle with the sesame seeds and serve with the lemon wedges.

These can be eaten on their own or added to a salad. Make a batch over the weekend and enjoy them all week! Chickpeas contain high amounts of manganese, which is essential for bone health.

ROASTED SPICED CHICKPEAS

SERVES: 4
PREP: 5 MINUTES
COOKING: 40 MINUTES

2 x 14-ounce cans chickpeas, drained and rinsed
2 tablespoons olive oil
1 tablespoon ground cumin
1 tablespoon chili powder
½ tablespoon cayenne pepper
½ tablespoon salt

Preheat the oven to 400°F.

Place the chickpeas in a large bowl and toss with the remaining ingredients until evenly coated. Spread the chickpeas in an even layer on a rimmed baking sheet and bake for 30 to 40 minutes until crisp. Store in an airtight container in the fridge for up to a week.

Feta is full of protein and is especially high in a mineral called chloride, which our bodies need to produce hydrochloric acid in the stomach, meaning you will break down and absorb other nutrients even better.

AVOCADO AND FETA ON SOURDOUGH

SERVES: 1
PREP: 5 MINUTES
COOKING: 2 MINUTES

1 slice of sourdough bread
1 avocado, peeled, pitted, and coarsely chopped
1 tablespoon lemon juice
salt and freshly ground black pepper
¼ cup feta cheese, crumbled

Toast the sourdough.

Meanwhile, mash the avocado, add the lemon juice, and season with salt and black pepper.

Once the sourdough is toasted, spread with the avocado and top with the feta.

To me, this snack is the taste of summer on a plate. Try and source as good-quality mozzarella as you can. Mozzarella contains vitamin B7, which can help your metabolism.

SLICED TOMATO AND MOZZARELLA

SERVES: 1
PREP: 5 MINUTES

4½ ounces good-quality mozzarella, sliced
1 large tomato, sliced
1 tablespoon extra virgin olive oil
salt and freshly ground black pepper
½ teaspoon dried oregano

Place the slices of mozzarella and tomato on a plate, drizzle with the oil, and season liberally with salt, pepper, and the oregano.

Try these addictive almonds as a quick snack. Almonds can lower blood-sugar levels, reduce blood pressure, and lower cholesterol. They can also reduce hunger and help to promote weight loss by making you feel fuller for longer.

CHILI-ROASTED ALMONDS

SERVES: 2
PREP: 1 MINUTES
COOKING: 5 MINUTES

2 cups whole almonds
1 tablespoon oil
1 to 2 teaspoons chili powder
1 teaspoon salt
1 tablespoon fresh lime juice
1 tablespoon chopped cilantro

Add the almonds and oil to a medium frying pan. Sprinkle with the chili powder and salt. Stir over medium heat for about 5 minutes until fragrant and toasted.

Remove the pan from heat and stir in the lime juice and cilantro. Transfer the nuts to a plate or baking sheet to cool. Store in an airtight container for up to a week.

These wraps will leave you feeling much more satisfied and there will be none of the bloating that can come with eating flour. Cottage cheese is one of the few dietary sources of vitamin D.

COTTAGE CHEESE AND TOMATO HAM WRAPS

SERVES: 2 TO 3
PREP: 5 MINUTES

1 cup cottage cheese
6 cherry tomatoes, diced
a handful of flat-leaf parsley, finely chopped
2 to 3 slices of good-quality ham
salt and freshly ground black pepper

Mix together the cottage cheese, tomatoes, and parsley and season with salt and pepper.

Lay out the slices of ham and place 2 tablespoons of the cheese mixture in the middle of each one. Fold in the sides and roll up to form a cigar shape. Store in an airtight container in the fridge.

HEALTHIER DESSERTS

Once you have weaned yourself off refined sugar you will start to appreciate naturally sweet tastes. Hopefully after having these delicious desserts you will realize you don't need the refined stuff! Enjoy these twice per week, on training days only, instead of having a snack between meals.

This is another one of my dad's recipes. Bust this out at a dinner party and see how amazed everyone is after finding out there is absolutely no added sugar in it.

TWO-INGREDIENT CHOCOLATE MOUSSE

SERVES: 2
PREP: 15 MINUTES

3½ ounces dark chocolate
3 large eggs, free range and preferably organic

Melt the chocolate, either in a microwave or in a heatproof bowl over a pan of simmering water, making sure the bowl doesn't directly touch the heat.

Separate the eggs. Lightly whisk the yolks using a fork and use an immersion blender to beat the egg whites until soft peaks form.

Remove the chocolate from the heat and set aside to cool at room temperature.

Once the chocolate has cooled a little, beat in the egg yolks, then fold the egg whites into the chocolate mixture (it can take a few minutes for it to look like a chocolate mousse).

Pour into small cups and chill in the fridge for 20 minutes. Serve with your choice of berries and cream.

Sometimes you may crave something sweet, so it pays to be organized and have these fudge squares ready and waiting for that moment. Don't get carried away though, as dates do contain a lot of natural sugar. A little bit now and then is fine! Peanut butter contains vitamin E, which can be used to improve your physical endurance. It can increase your energy and reduce the level of oxidative stress on your muscles after you exercise.

TWO-INGREDIENT PEANUT BUTTER FUDGE

MAKES: 12 SQUARES
PREP: 5 MINUTES

12 Medjool dates
1 cup natural peanut butter (no added sugar or oil)

Blend the dates and peanut butter in a food processor until the mixture turns into a ball. Press firmly into a 6 x 10-inch pan lined with parchment paper and freeze for 2 hours.

Cut into 12 squares, serve, and enjoy. Extras can be stored in an airtight container in the fridge for up to a week or the freezer for up to a month.

You may have seen these smoothie berry bowls all over social media. They taste great and are naturally sweet, so there's no need for added sugar. They should definitely be seen as a dessert though, not as a main meal. I nearly always have a stock of ripe frozen bananas in the freezer.

FROZEN BERRY SMOOTHIE BOWL

SERVES: 2
PREP: 5 MINUTES

1 cup organic frozen mixed berries, plus extra to serve (optional)
1 small ripe banana, sliced and frozen (2 hours in the freezer)
2 to 3 tablespoons light coconut or almond milk, plus more, as needed

Place the frozen berries and banana in a blender and blend on a slow speed until small bits remain.

Add the milk and blend on low again, scraping down the sides as needed, until the mixture reaches a soft consistency, making sure it's not too watery.

Scoop into serving bowls and top with more berries, if you wish.

I do love pancakes, but If I can help it I would rather not eat anything that is going to elevate my blood-sugar levels too much. These pancakes are made without flour, which means they will keep you fuller for longer but taste just as good!

BANANA CHOCOLATE PANCAKES

SERVES: 1
PREP: 5 MINUTES
COOKING: 15 MINUTES

1 banana, peeled and coarsely chopped
2 large eggs, free range and preferably organic
1 tablespoon cocoa powder
2 tablespoons grass-fed butter
a handful of raspberries
1 large tablespoon full-fat Greek yogurt
a drizzle of honey

Mash the banana until smooth. Whisk the eggs, then mix them with the mashed banana. Stir in the cocoa.

Melt the butter in a frying pan over medium heat. Add 2 tablespoons of the banana batter to the frying pan. It should sizzle immediately. Cook for 1 to 2 minutes until the bottom is brown when you lift the side. Flip the pancake (much more carefully than you would a regular pancake) and cook for another 1 to 2 minutes.

Serve with raspberries and Greek yogurt, and drizzle with honey.

This sounds incredibly decadent, but it isn't! This recipe makes the most out of the natural sweetness of its ingredients. Apples contain quercetin, a powerful antioxidant, which helps to fight the effects of inflammation and aging.

RAW CARAMEL APPLE COOKIES

SERVES: 2
PREP: 5 MINUTES

15 Medjool dates, soaked in water, until soft (about 5 minutes)
1 apple, skin on, cored and thickly sliced
2 tablespoons raisins
2 tablespoons unsweetened shredded coconut

In a food processor, blend the dates until they are finely chopped. Add ¼ cup water and blend again until the mixture turns into a paste.

Cut the apple into ¾ to 1½-inch circular slices and slather with the date paste.

Top with the raisins and sprinkle the coconut over the top.

The trick here is to use as good-quality dark chocolate as possible. You could use 100 percent cocoa and add a bit of honey. The flavanols in dark chocolate can stimulate the endothelium (the lining of arteries) to produce nitric oxide (NO), which is a gas. One of the functions of NO is to send signals to the arteries to relax, which lowers resistance to blood flow and therefore reduces blood pressure, making your workouts more effective.

RAW CHOCOLATE MACADAMIA BARK

SERVES: 8
PREP: 5 MINUTES
COOKING: 5 TO 10 MINUTES

10 ounces dark chocolate (approx. 85 to 90 percent cocoa solids), chopped into small pieces
2 handfuls of macadamia nuts, coarsely chopped
½ teaspoon sea salt

Heat two-thirds of the chocolate in the microwave or on the stove. If using a microwave, heat the chocolate in 30-second bursts, stirring vigorously between each burst. It should take 2 minutes or less to melt. If melting on the stove, create a double boiler by filling a saucepan with about an inch of water, and place a glass bowl with the chocolate in it just above the water. As the water gently boils, the steam will melt the chocolate without burning it. Stir occasionally, removing from heat as soon as the chocolate melts completely.

Stir the macadamia nuts into the chocolate.

Line a rimmed dish of your choice with parchment paper: the size of the dish will determine how thick the bark is.

Spread the chocolate evenly in the dish. Sprinkle with the salt. Chill for at least 10 minutes, or longer if the chocolate isn't solid yet. Use a knife to cut the bark into squares or misshapen pieces. Store in an airtight container at room temperature for a week.

This simple dessert tastes great on a warm summer's day, when you can use the freshest fruit possible. Peaches contain powerful antioxidants, which can help protect the body against the harmful effects of various diseases.

GRILLED FRUIT WITH HONEY AND RICOTTA

SERVES: 2
PREP: 5 MINUTES
COOKING: 5 MINUTES

1 tablespoon canola oil
2 plums, halved and pitted
2 peaches, halved and pitted
3 tablespoons full-fat ricotta cheese
honey, for drizzling

Heat a grill pan over high heat. Add the oil to the pan and grill the fruit, cut-side down, for 3 to 5 minutes until marked and softened. Serve with dollops of ricotta and drizzle with honey.

I love berries, especially when they are in season. They are very sweet, but contain far less natural sugar than many other fruits. Coconut cream contains up to 30 percent of your intake for magnesium, which is essential for muscle function.

SEASONAL BERRIES WITH COCONUT CREAM

SERVES: 2
PREP: 5 MINUTES

½ cup heavy cream
½ cup coconut cream
1½ cups mixed berries, such as raspberries, strawberries,
    or blackberries

Put the heavy cream and coconut cream in a bowl. Beat using an electric mixer until soft peaks form. Serve with the berries.

Dates are naturally sweet, so there is no need to add any kind of sweetener here. They are rich in magnesium, which means they are highly anti-inflammatory.

RAW CHOCOLATE BROWNIE

MAKES: 6
PREP: 15 MINUTES

2 cups whole walnuts
2¼ cups raw cacao
½ teaspoon sea salt
1 pound Medjool dates, pitted (about 18)
1½ cups unsalted almonds, coarsely chopped

Put the walnuts in a food processor and blend on high until finely ground. Add the cacao and salt. Pulse to combine.

Add the dates one at a time through the feed tube of the food processor while it is running. What you should end up with is a mixture that appears rather like cake crumbs, but that when pressed will easily stick together (if the mixture does not hold together well, add more dates).

In a large bowl (or the pan you plan on putting the brownies in), combine the walnut–cacao mixture with the almonds. Press into a 10-inch square cake pan or mold lined with parchment paper. Transfer to the freezer or fridge until ready to serve (it is also easier to cut these when they are very cold). Store in an airtight container for up to a week in the fridge.

The old saying, "If it sounds too good to be true, it probably is" doesn't apply to this dessert. There's no added sweetener, but it still tastes so chocolatey! Bananas contain pectin and resistant starch, which may moderate blood-sugar levels after meals and reduce appetite by slowing stomach emptying.

CHOCOLATE BANANA MILKSHAKE

SERVES: 1
PREP: 5 MINUTES

1 very ripe banana, peeled and frozen (2 hours in the freezer)
1¼ to 2 cups cow's milk or nut milk, such as almond, cashew, or coconut
1 tablespoon unsweetened cocoa powder

Blend all the ingredients together in a blender until smooth. Enjoy immediately.

CHAPTER 3

EXERCISE

Your body has a single purpose: to survive. To do that, it communicates with your environment via adaptation. Your environment imposes certain stresses on your body, and your body responds by adapting in a way that best suits its chances of survival.

Exercise is conscious communication with your body—you impose selected stress (exercise) on your body to sculpt your physique or improve your athletic performance. This adaptation occurs when you push yourself, so try to approach these workouts with 100 percent effort to transform your body into the leanest, fittest, and healthiest it can be.

EXERCISE

Having been involved in competitive sports at a high level nearly all my life, I understand what it takes to be in the best physical shape possible. I took part in national events for swimming, rugby, and athletics—I have never trained just for aesthetic reasons. Obviously, looking fit and healthy is great—it can boost confidence and help overcome insecurities. However, lots of the common problems people encounter with exercise, such as imbalances, injuries, and lack of mobility, stem from making looking good their only goal. Putting how you look rather than how you feel at the core of your training program can be counterproductive, especially if injury leads to extended periods of inactivity.

My workouts focus on getting stronger, faster, and fitter. Transforming how your body looks is a byproduct. I use a holistic approach to exercise, with mobility and flexibility drills to improve posture, imbalances, and help prevent injury.

Your reasons for exercising should be positive rather than negative: train because you love yourself, not because you hate yourself. Celebrate what your body can do, don't punish it for what you ate yesterday.

THE MIND/BODY CONNECTION

This is fundamental to my method of training. It's important to connect your mind and body when you are exercising, getting rid of all distractions and starting to feel your muscles work. Focus on consciously squeezing the muscles as you perform an exercise, at the same time as breathing deeply in a controlled way.

Exercising in this way has two benefits. Firstly, by focusing and consciously squeezing the target muscle, you make sure that you are activating the right muscles and deactivating the wrong ones. This vastly increases the efficiency of your workouts, which means that you will see results much quicker than if you were just going through the motions.

Secondly, training in this way helps you to be more mindful. Mindfulness is a mental state achieved by being aware of the present moment, forgetting about past emotions or future worries. This can be achieved by focusing on your bodily sensations during a workout.

This approach to training not only improves your physical health, but also your mental health by reducing stress, anxiety, and impulsivity, and improving concentration, optimism, and emotional intelligence.

QUALITY NOT QUANTITY

I believe that quality beats quantity when it comes to exercise. I think it is completely unnecessary to train more than four times a week; I average three sessions. People are often surprised by this, but in three sessions I give 110 percent—each rep is as close to perfect as possible in terms of technique, with absolute control activating all the right muscles. I keep things short, but the intensity high. It is not physically possible for me to train like this more than four times a week because my body needs the recovery days between sessions. On those recovery days I move as much as possible, stretch, and work on my mobility.

You will train the same way I, and all my clients do. Give 110 percent during your workouts and use your rest days for efficient recovery.

FASTED TRAINING

There is a whole host of benefits from training fasted (see pages 17–18). You accelerate the process of burning fat for energy, maximizing fat loss. Ideally, your workouts will be done in a fasted state, but this is not essential.

Workouts

There are two different types of workout: Resistance and HIIT (high-intensity interval training). For the duration of this plan you will do two of each a week.

Resistance training

Resistance work uses your own bodyweight, weights, or resistance bands to train your muscles. These exercises should be slow and controlled—remember to connect your mind and your body and feel all the muscles work as you move. If something doesn't feel hard enough, add some weight; you should be working toward using as heavy a weight as you can. Make sure you perfect the technique before attempting heavy weights. If you feel like the workout isn't hard enough, slow everything down and increase the weight.

There is a myth that lifting weights will make you "bulk up." I hear it all the time: "I don't want to get big" or "Can I not lift any weights please?" The "strong, not skinny" movement is slowly changing these misconceptions, but some people still think they will turn into The Hulk just by looking at a dumbbell.

The no. 1 goal for most of my female clients is to "tone up." What most of them don't realize is that to do so you need to do two things:

1. **Lose body fat** Everyone has abdominal muscles, but your body fat has to be low enough to be able to see them. You achieve a low body-fat percentage predominantly through what you eat. Intermittent fasting is a great way of accelerating the fat-burning process and therefore increasing your chances of having nicely toned abs.

2. **Build muscle** Achieving a low body-fat percentage without muscle definition is only half the battle. To get the toned look, you need to build muscle and the best way to do this is to lift weights.

The combination of fasting and weight training is very effective at transforming your physique. You will feel stronger, which can be empowering and can also reduce the risk of injuries and a lack of mobility in the long term.

HIIT (High-intensity interval training)

HIIT involves short-duration, MAXIMUM-effort exercise. These exercises should be performed as fast as possible. The aim is to get your heart rate as high as possible, improving fat-burning and increasing your metabolic rate for up to 24 hours after the workout.

HIIT hurts—but the average HIIT workout lasts only 20 minutes (including a warm-up and warm-down). It can take time to get used to exercising in this way, so you may feel light-headed and sometimes even a little nauseous. Don't worry, this is completely normal, and usually only happens during your first few HIIT sessions. If at any point you do feel faint, just increase your rest time until you start feeling normal again.

Rest days

Improving physical performance requires a two-pronged approach focusing on training and recovery. Each is as important as the other. Neglecting working on your flexibility, mobility, and stability during recovery can lead to problems later in life. As soon as you stop getting into certain positions or moving in certain ways, you can lose the ability to do so.

On your rest days, aim to move as much as possible and try my 5-minute movement sequence (see opposite).

WORKOUTS

You will perform four workouts per week: Two HIIT and two resistance sessions. On your recovery days, move as much as possible throughout the day and do the 5-minute movement sequence twice—first thing in the morning and right before bed.

WORKOUT SCHEDULE

4 workouts per week, alternating week by week:

	Week 1	Week 2	Week 3	Week 4
Monday	R1	R2	R1	R2
Tuesday	HIIT 1	HIIT 2	HIIT 1	HIIT 2
Wednesday	REST/MS	REST/MS	REST/MS	REST/MS
Thursday	HIIT 1	HIIT 2	HIIT 1	HIIT 2
Friday	REST/MS	REST/MS	REST/MS	REST/MS
Saturday	R1	R2	R1	R2
Sunday	REST/MS	REST/MS	REST/MS	REST/MS

5-MINUTE MOVEMENT SEQUENCE

To be done on your rest days 1 to 2 times. Put some effort into the stretches to improve flexibility. Breathe deeply throughout, staying as relaxed as possible.

1. Jumping Jacks – 30 seconds (page 174)
2. Standing Leg Swings – 10 each side (page 174)
3. Lying Towel Stretch – 30 seconds each side (page 177)
4. Deep Lunge – holding 30 seconds each side (page 175)
5. Deep Squat – 30 to 60 seconds (page 178)
6. Child's Pose – 30 seconds (page 179)
7. Arm Swings – 30 seconds (page 176)

WARM-UP – DYNAMIC MOVEMENTS

4 minutes

---

1. Jumping Jacks
(30 seconds)

- Start in a standing position, with your feet together and your hands by your sides.
- Jump so your feet move laterally and your straight arms are raised above your head.
- Land with your feet wider than shoulder-width apart and your hands touching directly above your head.
- Jump back into the starting position.

2. Standing Leg Swings
(30 seconds on each leg)

- Stand next to a wall or any stable surface you can lean on.
- Place one hand on the wall and the other on your hip.
- Swing your outside leg forward, keeping it straight; you will feel a stretch in your hamstring at the back of your thigh. Aim to keep your hips completely still by placing one hand on your hip and controlling the motion.
- Repeat this process, gradually increasing the height of the straight leg each time, without forcing it. Do put some effort into it: imagine you are trying to kick a ball hard.
- Turn around and repeat on the other side.

3. Deep Lunge (30 seconds, switching every 2 to 3 seconds)

- Start in the plank position, with your straight arms underneath your shoulders and your whole body straight, resting on your toes.
- Bring one foot as far forward as you can and place it flat on the outside of the hand on the same side.
- Drop your hips and hold that position for 2 to 3 seconds.
- Return your leg to the starting position and repeat on the other side.

4. Glute Raises (30 seconds on each leg)

- Lie on your side, resting your head on your hand and tilting your hips toward the floor.
- Engage your top glute (squeeze your top bum cheek) and raise the top leg up as high as you can, but keep your toes pointing down toward the floor.
- Lower the leg back down and repeat.
- Repeat on the other side.

Note: You need to constantly squeeze your glute as you raise your leg up for this to work properly.

5. Ab Activation
(30 seconds)

- Lie flat on your back, with your arms extended by your sides and your knees bent with your feet flat.
- Bring your chin in toward your chest, exhale, and reach as far forward as possible with your extended arms—imagine you are trying to reach for something in front of you—but keep your lower back flat and tense your abdominals as hard as you can.
- Hold at the top of the movement for 3 seconds.
- Very slowly, lower yourself back down, gradually releasing the tension in your abs.

6. Arm Swings (30 seconds)

- Start in a standing position with your feet shoulder-width apart.
- Swing your straight arms back behind you, with the movement coming from the shoulders.
- Swing your arms forward, so your arms cross over in front of you.
- Repeat this motion, alternating which arm goes on top as they cross in front.
- The speed and range of movement should be increased gradually.

WARM-DOWN – STATIC POSITIONS

5 minutes

1. Lying Glute Stretch
(30 seconds on each leg)

- Lie flat on your back on the floor with your feet flat and knees pointing toward the ceiling.
- Cross one leg over the other, so one knee is pointing to the side.
- Grab hold of the top knee and your shin.
- Pull your knee in toward your chest, at the same time as pushing with the bottom leg.
- Repeat on the other side.

2. Lying Towel Stretch
(30 seconds on each leg)

- Grab a towel or something you can wrap around your foot and hold on to. A resistance band would be ideal, if you have one.
- Keeping your back and head flat on the floor, pull your straight leg up toward your chest.
- Pull quite hard with your arms and hold at the point where you can't go any further.
- Breathe deeply, increasing the stretch on every exhale.
- Repeat on the other side.

3. Deep Lunge
(page 175)

4. Deep Squat (30 seconds)

- Stand with your feet slightly wider than shoulder-width apart.
- Drop down as low as you can into a deep squat, keeping your feet flat.
- Keep your chest up and place your hands into a prayer position, so that your elbows are pushing out on your knees.
- Push your knees out with your elbows as hard as you can. To make it harder you can bring your hands into fists, pressing in on each other.
- If you can't get into that position without your heels lifting, place a book or something similar underneath each heel, so you can rest them on something. As you get better at this move, you will gradually be able to lower your heels so they are flat.

5. Child's Pose (30 seconds)

- Kneel with your feet together behind you and your knees open wide.
- Bend over so that your straight arms are resting on the floor and you are reaching as far forward as you can.
- Lower your chest toward the floor, keeping your arms completely straight.
- Hold that position, twisting your torso from side to side from your hips.

6. Standing Inner Thigh Stretch (30 seconds on each leg)

- Stand with your feet wide apart, both pointing forward.
- Bend one leg and push your hips to the side of the bent leg.
- Lean to the side of your straight leg to increase the stretch.
- Repeat on the other side.

RESISTANCE 1

Perform slowly and with control—33 minutes (including 9 minutes for both the warm-up and warm-down).

>> Warm-up (pages 174–176)

Group 1: *45 seconds of each exercise, repeated 4 times with 15 seconds' rest in between each one.*

1. Glute Bridge

- Lie down flat on the floor and rest your heels on something raised with your knees bent.
- Exhale and push through your heels to raise your hips until you make a straight line down your body from your knees to your shoulders.
- Inhale, slowly lowering your hips back down to the floor.

2a. Push-ups – kneeling

- Start on all fours, with your hands directly underneath your shoulders. Get your back as flat as possible by tilting your hips upward toward your belly button.
- Inhale as you bend your elbows back and let your chest drop toward the floor, keeping your hips tilted upward, so that your abdominals are engaged. Go as low as you can.
- Exhale as you push back up.

2b. Push-ups – full

- Start in the full plank position. Keep the abdominals/core engaged.
- Inhale as you bend your elbows back and let your chest drop toward the floor, keeping your hips tilted upward, so that your abdominals are engaged. Go as low as you can.
- Exhale as you push back up, extending your arms and squeezing your triceps and chest muscles as you push up.

3. Hollow Hold

- Start flat on your back, placing your hands behind your head and bringing your knees in toward your chest.
- Lift your chest off the floor using your abdominal muscles, and extend your legs straight up toward the ceiling or sky. Lock your knees and point your toes.
- Keeping your chest lifted off the floor using your abs, lower your straight legs down toward the floor, making sure your lower back does not arch. (The lower your legs go, the harder your abdominals have to work; if your abs aren't strong enough, your back will want to take the strain.)
- Find the angle in which you can hold this pose without your lower back arching, all the time lifting your chest off the floor to create the hollow body position.

Group 2: *45 seconds of each exercise, repeated 4 times with 15 seconds' rest in between each one.*

4. Squats (dumbbell optional)

- Stand with your feet shoulder-width apart; push your bottom back, keeping your chest up.
- Inhale as you drop your bottom down, as if you are trying to tap it on an invisible chair. At the same time raise your arms up so the weight is just in front of your chest, all the time keeping your chest facing forward and your weight on your heels.
- Exhale as you drive through your heels as you stand up squeezing your glutes together until you are fully standing up.
- If you are holding a weight, hold it with both palms pointing upward with the weight resting on the palms of your hands.

5. Toe Touches
(dumbbell optional)

- Lie flat on your back on the floor, with your toes pointing toward the ceiling and your knees locked.
- Point your hands toward your toes, exhale, and use your abdominals to reach with your hands toward your feet.
- Inhale as you slowly lower your torso back toward the floor, but keep your hands pointing toward your toes and don't let your upper back and neck touch the floor. Repeat this process.
- If using a dumbbell, hold it with both hands as you perform this exercise.

6. Shoulder Press
(with dumbbells)

- Stand with your feet shoulder-width apart and your hands by your shoulders, elbows pointing down and palms facing forward.
- Keep your abdominals engaged as you exhale and push the weights up above your head, until your arms are fully extended.
- Inhale as you slowly bend your elbows back and lower the weights back to the starting position.

>> Warm-down (page 177–179)

RESISTANCE 2

Perform slowly and with control—33 minutes (including 9 minutes for both the warm-up and warm-down).

>> Warm-up (page 174–176)

Group 1: *45 seconds of each exercise, repeated 4 times with 15 seconds' rest in between each one.*

1. Static Lunge (dumbbells optional)

- Start with one foot behind you and one slightly in front with about 3 feet in between.
- As you inhale, drop your back knee down, but don't let it touch the floor. Keep your torso upright as you do this, and make sure your front knee stays behind your front toe.
- Exhale as you push back up through both legs, back into the starting position.
- If you are using dumbbells, hold one in each hand with straight arms pointing toward the floor.

2. Bench Dips

- Find a bench or a chair with a surface about 3 feet off the floor.
- Place your hands on the bench or chair so your fingers are wrapped over the front edge and your palms are resting on the top.
- One at a time, extend your legs out straight in front of you—the straighter you have your legs, the harder this exercise will be.
- Inhale as you bend your elbows back, allowing your body to drop toward the floor as you do so.
- Exhale as you squeeze your triceps and push yourself back up into the starting position, locking your arms at the top.

3. Hollow Plank

- Start in a normal plank position, but then rock your body slightly forward so all the weight is on your arms and you are on your tiptoes.
- Constantly tilt your hips toward your belly button and squeeze your glutes to engage your abs.
- Push yourself away from the floor, so your shoulder blades are pushed into your back.
- Hold this position actively for the duration. Don't relax halfway through.

Group 2: *45 seconds of each exercise, repeated 4 times with 15 seconds' rest in between each one.*

4. Squat Press (with dumbbells)

- Stand with your feet shoulder-width apart and a dumbbell in each hand, held at your chest.
- Inhale as you push your bottom back, keeping your chest up. Then drop your bottom down, as if you are trying to tap it on an invisible chair.
- Exhale as you drive through your heels to stand up, squeezing your glutes together and raising the weights up into a shoulder press.
- As you come back down into the next squat, bring your arms down, so the weights are in front of your chest again.

5. Russian Twist (with dumbbell)

- Sit down on your bottom with your knees bent toward your chest, feet flat on the floor, and one dumbbell held with both hands.
- Contract your abdominals and lean back about 45 degrees, keeping your abs engaged.
- Once you are in position, twist your torso from side to side, squeezing your oblique muscles at the side of your abdominals as you move and always engaging your abs.
- If you want to make it harder, repeat exactly the same movement with your feet off the floor.

6. Lying Leg Raises

- Start lying flat on your back, placing your hands underneath your lower back.
- Bring your knees in toward your chest, then extend them upward, locking your knees and pointing your toes.
- As you exhale, lower your straight legs down toward the floor, going as low as possible and squeezing your abdominals as you do.
- Inhale as you slowly bring your legs back up to the starting position.
- To make this harder, take your hands away from your back, but make sure that you keep your lower back flat against the floor as you lower your legs.

▶▶ Warm-down (pages 177–179)

HIIT 1

Perform as many repetitions as you can as fast as possible—29 minutes (including 9 minutes for both the warm-up and warm-down).

>> Warm-up (pages 174–176)

45 seconds of each exercise, repeated 5 times with 15 seconds' rest in between exercises and 30 seconds' rest between each round.

1. Burpees

- Start in a standing position, then jump into the air.
- As you land on your feet, move your hands toward the floor and hurl your legs back so you are in a push-up/plank position, making sure your back isn't sagging toward the floor.
- Jump straight out of that position by bringing your feet back under your hips and then extending your legs and your torso upward, leaping into the air in one movement.
- Repeat this movement as fast as possible.

2. Mountain Climbers

- Start in the plank position with most of your weight on your upper body, making sure your shoulders are slightly in front of your hands. (There should be as little weight as possible on your feet, so you can move them easily.)
- Start bringing one knee as close to your chest as possible. As you start returning your leg to the starting position, start bringing the other knee in toward your chest.
- This should be done very fast. Your legs should be the only things moving; your hips stay absolutely still and your torso should be still, with all the weight distributed toward your arms.

3. Jumping Jacks

- Start in a standing position, with your feet together and your hands by your sides.
- Jump so your feet move laterally and your straight arms are raised above your head.
- Land with your feet wider than shoulder-width apart and your hands touching directly above your head.
- Jump back into the starting position.

4. High Knees

- Start in a standing position, with your feet together and your hands by your sides.
- Drive one arm and the opposite knee up, so that your knee is level with your hip.
- Repeat on the other side as the first side returns to the starting position.
- Do this as fast as you can. The more you drive your arms, the faster your legs will go.

>> Warm-down (pages 177–179)

HIIT 2

Perform as many repetitions as you can as fast as possible—29 minutes (including 9 minutes for both the warm-up and warm-down).

>> Warm-up (pages 174–176)

45 seconds of each exercise, repeated 5 times with 15 seconds' rest in between exercises and 30 seconds' rest between each round.

1. Squat Jumps

- Stand with your feet shoulder-width apart and push your bottom back, keeping your chest up.
- Inhale as you drop your bottom down, as if you are trying to tap it on an invisible chair, and at the same time bring your arms into your chest, all the time keeping your chest facing forward and your weight on your heels.
- Exhale as you jump straight up, extending your arms toward the floor and pointing your toes toward the floor as well.
- Land in a squat with your hands in at your chest again and repeat.

2. Plank In and Outs

- Start in the plank position, but resting on your elbows rather than your palms.
- Jump out with your feet, so you land on your toes with your feet wider than your shoulders. Keep the rest of your body absolutely still.
- Jump back into the starting position and repeat.
- Do this movement quickly, but try to keep your hips still by keeping your core engaged the whole time.

3. Tuck Jumps

- Start with your feet together and your hands in front of your abdomen.
- Jump up, bringing your knees toward your hands.
- As soon as your feet touch the floor, jump straight back up again.
- This should be done very fast, with virtually no contact time on the floor.

4. Squat Thrusts

- Start in the plank position with most of your weight on your upper body, making sure your shoulders are slightly in front of your hands. (There should be as little weight as possible on your feet, so you can move them easily.)
- Bring both knees in toward your chest and land on your tiptoes in that position, keeping your hips still.
- Jump back out into the starting position, landing on your toes again.
- Aim to keep your hips and your torso still and just move your legs.

>> Warm-down (pages 177–179)

INDEX

aging, slowing 17
alcohol 29–30
almond butter, apple with 140
almonds, chili-roasted 148
anchovies, grilled zucchini salad
   with 87
apples: apple with almond butter 140
   raw caramel apple cookies 159
asparagus: crunchy Asian asparagus
   salad 103
avocados: avocado and feta on
   sourdough 147
     avocado pesto spaghetti 54
     egg guacamole goodness bowl 82
     Mexican sweet potato skins
      with guacamole 48
     tuna guacamole 134

bacon: chicken with creamy bacon
   mushroom sauce 91
     classic bacon and poached
      eggs 77
     creamy goat cheese spaghetti
      with bacon 51
     mushrooms and bacon on toast 47
     trout with bacon and peas 123
bananas: banana chocolate
   pancakes 158
     chocolate banana milkshake 167
     peanut butter and banana on
      rye 140
bark, raw chocolate macadamia 161
beans, one-pan chorizo with 113
beef: beef stroganoff 94
     breakfast burritos 46
     honey-glazed sesame beef 61
     Mexican cheese steak melt 42
     round steak with herb
      vinaigrette 127
beets: baked beet, walnut,
   and goat cheese salad 96
     beet hummus 143
berries: frozen berry smoothie bowl 156
     summer berries with coconut
      cream 164
body fat, losing 172
bread: avocado and feta on
   sourdough 147
     Mexican cheese steak melt 42
     mushrooms and bacon on toast 47
     peanut butter and banana on
      rye 140

breakfast burritos 46
brownies, raw chocolate 165
burgers, teriyaki turkey 95
burritos, breakfast 46
butternut squash, fish casserole 65

caramel apple cookies, raw 159
carbohydrates 24–25
cashew butter: creamy cashew soba
   noodles 38
casserole, tuna 55
cheese: avocado and feta on
     sourdough 147
     baked beet, walnut, and
      goat cheese salad 96
     blue-cheese-stuffed portobello
      mushrooms 100
     cottage cheese and tomato
      ham wraps 146
     creamy goat cheese
      spaghetti 51
     creamy mushroom and
      Parmesan risotto 52
     eggplant parmigiana 114
     feta and sun-dried tomato dip 134
     goat cheese and tomato
      pesto frittata 83
     pork tenderloin with creamy
      goat cheese sauce 88
     Mexican cheese steak melt 42
     mozzarella chicken 58
     sliced tomato and mozzarella 147
     sweet potato, pine nut, and feta
      salad 57
     see also ricotta cheese
chicken: chicken and sun-dried
   tomato pesto zucchini noodles 124
     chicken breast with a lemon
      yogurt sauce 107
     chicken with creamy bacon
      mushroom sauce 91
     mozzarella chicken 58
     smoky chicken skewers 144
     soy and honey-glazed chicken 41
     Thai green chicken curry 99
chickpeas: mackerel with chickpeas 66
     roasted spiced chickpeas 144
chiles: chile-covered salmon 110
     chili-roasted almonds 148
chocolate: banana chocolate
   pancakes 158
     chocolate banana milkshake 167
     chocolate mousse 152
     raw chocolate brownie 165
     raw chocolate macadamia

     bark 161
chorizo with beans, one-pan 113
coconut cream, summer berries
   with 164
coconut milk: coconut rice 41
cookies, raw caramel apple 159
cottage cheese and tomato
   ham wraps 148
curry: shrimp and tomato curry 104
     Thai green chicken curry 99

dips: eggplant dip 137
     feta and sun-dried tomato dip 134
diabetes 16
diseases, reducing risk of 17

eggplant: eggplant dip 137
     eggplant mini pizzas 92
     eggplant parmigiana 114
eggs: baked kale and eggs 81
     breakfast burritos 46
     classic bacon and poached
      egg with a twist 77
     deviled eggs 141
     egg guacamole goodness bowl 82
     goat cheese and tomato
      pesto frittata 83
     mushroom omelet 74
     shakshuka 120
     smoked salmon mini frittatas 78
energy levels, stable 15–16
exercise 17–18, 168–189

fasting 11, 13, 18
     benefits of 15–17
fat 24
fish: fish casserole 65
     see also salmon; tuna, etc
frittatas: goat cheese and tomato
   pesto frittata 83
     smoked salmon mini frittatas 78
fruit: grilled fruit with honey and
   ricotta 162
fudge, peanut butter 155

garlic pesto 118
gnocchi: baked tomato gnocchi 71
guacamole 48
     egg guacamole goodness bowl 82
     tuna guacamole 134

ham, cottage cheese and tomato
   ham wraps 148
HIIT 172, 186–189
hummus, beet 143

hunger, reduced 16

immune system, improving 17
insulin sensitivity, improved 16–17
Italian lamb chops 109

kale: baked kale and eggs 81

lamb chops, Italian 109
lettuce cups, tuna 106

macadamia bark, raw chocolate 161
mackerel: baked mackerel and
    garlic pesto 118
        mackerel with chickpeas and a
            basil and lemon dressing 66
        smoked mackerel pâté 138
macronutrients 23–25
meal plans 32–35
Mediterranean salad 114
metabolism 18
Mexican cheese steak melt 42
Mexican sweet potato skins 48
milkshake, chocolate banana 167
mind/body connection 171
mousse, chocolate 152
muscles 18, 172
mushrooms: blue-cheese-stuffed
    portobello mushrooms 100
        chicken with creamy bacon
            mushroom sauce 91
        creamy goat cheese spaghetti
            with mushrooms 51
        creamy mushroom and
            Parmesan risotto 52
        mushroom omelet 74
        mushrooms and bacon on toast 47

noodles: creamy cashew soba
    noodles 38
        honey-glazed sesame beef
            with soba noodles 61

omelet, mushroom 74

pancakes, banana chocolate 158
pancetta: scallops with spinach and 117
parmigiana, eggplant 114
pasta: avocado pesto spaghetti 54
    creamy goat cheese spaghetti 51
pâté, smoked mackerel 138
peanut butter: peanut butter and
    banana on rye 140
        peanut butter fudge 155
        pork chop with peanut butter

satay 131
peas, trout with bacon and 123
pesto: avocado pesto spaghetti 54
    chicken and sun-dried tomato
        pesto zucchini noodles 124
    garlic pesto 118
    goat cheese and tomato
        pesto frittata 83
    tomato pesto quinoa with
        spinach 69
pine nuts: creamed Swiss chard with
    pine nuts 121
        sweet potato, pine nut, and feta
            salad 57
pizzas, eggplant mini 92
pork: pork tenderloin with creamy
    goat cheese sauce 88
        pork chop with peanut butter
            satay 131
protein 24

quinoa: tomato pesto quinoa with
    spinach 69

resistance training 172, 180–185
rice: creamy mushroom and
    Parmesan risotto 52
        soy and honey-glazed chicken
            with coconut rice 41
        spiced rice 62
ricotta, grilled fruit with honey and 162

salads: Asian slaw 131
    baked beet, walnut, and
        goat cheese salad 96
    crunchy Asian asparagus salad 103
    grilled zucchini salad 87
    Mediterranean salad 114
    shrimp salad in a jar 84
    sweet potato, pine nut, and feta
        salad 57
salmon: chile-covered salmon with
    spinach 110
        salmon goodness bowl 45
        smoked salmon mini frittatas 78
satay, pork chop with peanut butter
    131
scallops with pancetta and spinach 117
sea bass with sauce vierge 128
shakshuka 120
shrimp: shrimp and tomato curry 104
    shrimp salad in a jar 84
skewers, smoky chicken 144
smoothie bowl, frozen berry 156
spinach: chile-covered salmon with 110

creamy goat cheese spaghetti
    with spinach, bacon, and
    mushrooms 51
scallops with pancetta and
    spinach 117
sea bass with sauce vierge 128
tomato pesto quinoa with 69
stroganoff, beef 94
supplements 25
sweet potatoes: Mexican sweet
    potato skins 48
        sweet potato, pine nut, and feta
            salad 57
Swiss chard: creamed Swiss chard
    with pine nuts 121
        round steak with chard 127

teriyaki turkey burgers 95
Thai green chicken curry 99
tomatoes: chicken and sun-dried
    tomato pesto zucchini noodles 124
        baked tomato gnocchi 71
        cottage cheese and tomato
            ham wraps 148
        eggplant parmigiana 114
        feta and sun-dried tomato dip 134
        goat cheese and tomato
            pesto frittata 83
        sea bass with sauce vierge 128
        shakshuka 120
        shrimp and tomato curry 104
        sliced tomato and mozzarella 147
        tomato pesto quinoa with
            spinach 69
trout with bacon and peas 123
tuna: seared tuna and crunchy Asian
    asparagus salad 103
        tuna casserole 55
        tuna guacamole 134
        tuna lettuce cups 106
turkey burgers, teriyaki 95

walnuts: baked beet, walnut,
    and goat cheese salad 96
weight loss 15
workouts 172–173

yogurt: chicken breast with a lemon
    yogurt sauce 107
        Greek yogurt with honey and
            ginger 141

zucchini: chicken and sun-dried
    tomato pesto zucchini noodles 124
        grilled zucchini salad 87

2 meal day®

Your body is an intelligent machine, let's treat it this way.

Get your tailored plan and start your transformation by visiting **www.2mealday.com**